U. S. FOREIGN POLICY:

Shield of the Republic

U. S. FOREIGN POLICY:

Shield of the Republic

By

WALTER LIPPMANN

AN ATLANTIC MONTHLY PRESS BOOK

LITTLE, BROWN AND COMPANY · BOSTON

1943

ATLANTIC–LITTLE, BROWN BOOKS
ARE PUBLISHED BY
LITTLE, BROWN AND COMPANY
IN ASSOCIATION WITH
THE ATLANTIC MONTHLY PRESS

PRINTED AND BOUND IN THE U. S. A. BY
KINGSPORT PRESS, INC., KINGSPORT, TENN.

To
H. B. L.

ACKNOWLEDGMENTS

I AM specially indebted to Edward Weeks, the editor of the *Atlantic Monthly*, for encouragement while writing this book, for his editorial guidance, and his criticism of the text; to Miss Frances Van Schaick, who assisted me in assembling the material and at all stages in the preparation of the manuscript; to Dean Paul H. Buck of Harvard University and to Professor Ruhl J. Bartlett of Tufts College for their constructive suggestions; to Mr. Robert Wolff, for his very helpful criticism of the text; and to my wife, for her advice.

It is impossible for me here to acknowledge my indebtedness to all the books I have read, to all the public men here and abroad I have talked with, to all the journalists and editors whose work I have drawn upon in the course of thirty years. I am reserving that pleasure for the quiet evenings when the storms of our days are spent.

INTRODUCTION

FOR a very special reason a few words of explanation are needed by way of introduction to this book. My main thesis is that the foreign policy which had served the United States, on the whole so well, during most of the nineteenth century became dangerously inadequate after 1900. Then the United States expanded its commitments into Asiatic waters by the occupation of the Philippines, and then Germany, by deciding to build a great navy, emerged from continental Europe as a challenger for world power. I shall be arguing in this book that because of our failure to readjust the foreign policy of the United States to this revolutionary change in the situation, the nation has for over forty years been unprepared to wage war or to make peace, and has remained divided within itself on the conduct of American foreign relations.

The argument, as the reader will see, becomes a severe criticism of American policy during this period. Since I have lived through this period, and have for thirty years been writing books and articles about current events, I have been troubled because, with the advantages of hindsight, I am criticizing others for holding views which at the time I may myself have shared, or for a lack of foresight of which I was also guilty. Therefore, I should like to make it as plain as possible at the outset that nothing could be further from my intention than to say to anyone that I told him so. For the conclusions which I have set down in this book are drawn from experience. I was not born with them. I have come to them slowly over thirty years, and as a result of many false starts, mistaken judgments, and serious disappointments. They represent what I now think I have learned, not at all what I always knew.

Yet in writing the book during the summer of 1942 and the winter of 1943 I could not stop to confess as I went along how on this point or that I had at some earlier time thought differently. Confession may be good for the soul. But when our urgent business is to make up our minds on what is for the best interests of the country, it would have been as conceited as it was boring to annotate the argument with a running history of my own previous opinions.

Now that the book is done I am much better aware than I was before writing it how wide has been the gap between my own insight and my own hindsight. Thus I cannot remember taking any interest whatsoever in foreign affairs until after the outbreak of the first World War. As a boy I had, to be sure, been greatly excited by the sinking of the battleship *Maine* and by Dewey's victory in Manila Bay and by the battle of Santiago, and from my grandfather who hated Prussia I had acquired the conviction that wherever the American flag was planted, there tyranny must disappear. But years afterwards, in spite of college and much reading about public affairs, I remained quite innocent of any understanding of the revolutionary consequences of the Spanish-American War.

In fact I came out of college thinking that Theodore Roosevelt, whom I admired profoundly, was in this respect eccentric, that he kept harping on the Panama Canal and the navy. For in my youth we all assumed that the money spent on battleships would better be spent on schoolhouses, and that war was an affair that "militarists" talked about and not something that seriously-minded progressive democrats paid any attention to. So when my teacher, Graham Wallas, warned me, as I was leaving Harvard in 1910, that a great war might soon break out and that if it did, it would probably smoulder on for thirty years, I had no notion that it would ever touch me or jeopardize the interests of the country.

It was possible for an American in those days to be totally unconscious of the world he lived in. Thus I took ship and sailed for England a few days after the Archduke Ferdinand was assassinated at Sarajevo in June 1914, and I spent a delightful month of July in London and then in the English Lake country where I attended a summer school presided over by the Webbs and by Bernard Shaw. I do not remember hearing any discussion of the Serbian crisis, and so little concern did I have with it that in the last week of July I crossed over to Belgium, loitered at Ostend and Bruges and Ghent, went on to Brussels and then bought a ticket for a journey through Germany to Switzerland, where I meant to spend my vacation walking over mountain passes. I remember being astonished and rather annoyed when I went to the railroad station and found that the German border was closed because Belgium had had an ultimatum.

So I know at least one young man who was not mentally prepared for the age he was destined to live in. Nor even under the shock of one great war did an understanding come to him easily. I began to take foreign affairs seriously on August 4, 1914, when, having returned to England from Belgium, I was in the House of Commons lobby when Britain declared war. For two years, thereafter, in association with Herbert Croly, I struggled with misgiving and reluctance to grasp our interest in the war. Thus I had learned to understand, even before 1917, that a German victory through the submarine blockade would be a triumph of the Prussian military caste "which aims to make Germany the leader of the East against the West, the leader ultimately of a German-Russian-Japanese coalition against the Atlantic world." But though later I worked for President Wilson under Colonel House's direction on the terms of peace, I did not have the sense to see that the acquisition of the German islands in the Pacific north of the equator by Japan was a fatal blow to our defenses in the Pacific.

And though I knew, and had often argued, that British-American sea power combined was necessary to our own security and to the maintenance of peace, nevertheless I was too weak-minded to take a stand against the exorbitant folly of the Washington Disarmament Conference. In fact, I followed the fashion, and in editorials for the old *New York World* celebrated the disaster as a triumph and denounced the admirals who dared to protest. Of that episode in my life I am ashamed, all the more so because I had no excuse for not knowing better.

So the reader will, I hope, feel that I have said quite enough about myself to discount any suggestion in what follows that I see the mote in my brother's eye and not the beam in mine own.

W. L.

Washington, D. C.
March 6, 1943

CONTENTS

Contents

PART ONE

. . . When we may choose peace or war, as our interest, guided by justice, shall counsel.

— GEORGE WASHINGTON
The Farewell Address, September 17, 1796

CHAPTER I

THE SUBJECT OF THIS BOOK

As THE climax of the war finds the people of the United States approaching a national election, we must face the fact that for nearly fifty years the nation has not had a settled and generally accepted foreign policy. This is a danger to the Republic. For when a people is divided within itself about the conduct of its foreign relations, it is unable to agree on the determination of its true interest. It is unable to prepare adequately for war or to safeguard successfully its peace. Thus its course in foreign affairs depends, in Hamilton's words, not on reflection and choice but on accident and force.

The country, as I shall try to demonstrate, had a secure foreign policy toward the great powers from the decade after the end of the War of 1812 to the end of the war with Spain in 1898. In that long period it was true that politics stopped at the water's edge, and that the people were not seriously divided on our relations with the Old World. But in the election of 1900 the nation became divided over the consequences of the war with Spain, and never since then has it been possible for any President of the United

States to rely upon the united support of the nation in the conduct of foreign affairs.

The consequences have been grave. The war with Spain left the United States with commitments in the Pacific 7000 miles west of California. The lack of a settled foreign policy made it impossible for the United States to liquidate the commitment by withdrawing from the Far Pacific or to fulfill the commitment by assuring the defense of the Philippines. The outbreak of the first World War in Europe precipitated an internal controversy in the United States about America's rights and its interests, its duties and its obligations. As a result of that division of opinion the country was unable to prepare for that war even when American participation had become probable, and it was unable to consolidate the victory which it helped to win. During the twenty years which followed there was unending domestic controversy over foreign policy. This made the American government as ineffective in preventing the second World War as it was in preparing for it. Now, under the spell cast by the coming elections of 1944, the country again finds itself unable to think clearly and to decide firmly what policy it will follow in the settlement of the war.

The spectacle of this great nation which does not know its own mind is as humiliating as it is dangerous. It casts doubt upon the capacity of the people to govern themselves. For nowhere else on earth, and never before in all history, has any people had conditions so favorable as they are in the United States to proving their capacity for self-government. It will be a profound humiliation, therefore, if once again we fail to form a national policy, and the acids of this failure will be with us for ages to come, corroding our self-confidence and our self-respect. Our failure now to form a national policy will, though we defeat our enemies, leave us dangerously exposed to deadly conflict at home and to unmanageable perils from abroad. For the return from a state of total war to a state of peace which no one trusts will raise catastrophic issues in our midst. Rent by domestic controversy, for want of a settled foreign policy we shall act not upon reflection and choice but under the impulse of accidents and the impact of force.

In pondering our failure to form a foreign policy in the twentieth century, we must remember that each of us is himself susceptible to the partisanship which is the cause of that failure. Therefore, we must shun the temptation to explain on the ground that they are stupid, ambitious, or self-regarding the opposition of those who have differed with us.

Candor, as Hamilton said in beginning his argument for the adoption of the Constitution, will oblige us to admit that, in this half century of controversy, "wise and good men" have been "on the wrong as well as on the right side of questions of the first magnitude to society," and that "we are not always sure that those who advocate the truth are influenced by purer principles than their antagonists," and that "ambition, avarice, personal animosity and party opposition, and many other motives not more laudable than these, are apt to operate as well upon those who support, as upon those who oppose, the right side of a question."

More than charity of mind and humility of soul dictates this approach to the settlement of our national division. An objective study of our foreign relations in the past fifty years will, I believe, show that our national failure to form a foreign policy is due to an historic circumstance. For about eighty years — from the promulgation of the Monroe Doctrine to the end of the war with Spain — there was no need for the American people to form a foreign policy. In that long period the very nature of foreign policy, of what it consists and how it is formed, was forgotten. Thus, when events compelled us once again to attend to foreign relations, we had lost the art of shaping a policy, and could not find a policy because we no longer knew what we needed.

This is the reason why good and patriotic Americans have differed so sharply and so long without reaching a common view. They have forgotten the compelling and, once seen, the self-evident common principle of all genuine foreign policy — the principle that alone can force decisions, can settle controversy, and can induce agreement. This is the principle that in foreign relations, as in all other relations, a policy has been formed only when commitments and power have been brought into balance. This is the forgotten principle which must be recovered and restored to the first place in American thought if the nation is to achieve the foreign policy which it so desperately wants.

Without the controlling principle that the nation must maintain its objectives and its power in equilibrium, its purposes within its means and its means equal to its purposes, its commitments related to its resources and its resources adequate to its commitments, it is impossible to think at all about foreign affairs. Yet the history of our acts and of our declarations in the past fifty years will show that rarely, and never consistently, have American statesmen and the American people been guided by this elementary principle of practical life.

No one would seriously suppose that he had a fiscal policy if he did not consider together expenditure and revenue, outgo and income, liabilities and assets. But in foreign relations we have habitually in our minds divorced the discussion of our war aims, our peace aims, our ideals, our interests, our commitments, from the discussion of our armaments, our strategic position, our potential allies and our probable enemies. No policy could emerge from such a discussion. For what settles practical controversy is the knowledge that ends and means have to be balanced: an agreement has eventually to be reached when men admit that they must pay for what they want and that they must want only what they are willing to pay for. If they do not have to come to such an agreement, they will never except by accident agree. For they will lack a yard-stick by which to measure their ideals and their interests, or their ways and means of protecting and promoting them.

If we survey, as we shall in the course of the argument, our own course since the war with Spain, we shall find that there has been no serious and sustained conviction that American commitments and interests and ideals must be covered by our armaments, our strategic frontiers, and our alliances. In fact we shall find that we have been the victims of a blinding prejudice — that concern with our frontiers, our armaments, and with alliances, is immoral and reactionary.

Yet now that the Philippines have been lost, now that we have been attacked by a combination of exceedingly dangerous enemies, we must see how awful is the price we must pay because in our foreign relations for nearly half a century the United States has been insolvent. This is the time of the reckoning. We are liquidating in sweat and blood and tears, and at our mortal peril, the fact that we made commitments, asserted rights, and proclaimed ideals while we left our frontiers unguarded, our armaments unprepared, and our alliances unformed and unsustained.

CHAPTER II

THE FUNDAMENTAL PRINCIPLE OF A FOREIGN POLICY

BEFORE we examine the history of our insolvent foreign relations, we must be sure that we know what we mean by a foreign commitment and by the power to balance it.

I mean by a *foreign commitment* an obligation, outside the continental limits of the United States, which may in the last analysis have to be met by waging war.

I mean by *power* the force which is necessary to prevent such a war or to win it if it cannot be prevented. In the term *necessary* power I include the military force which can be mobilized effectively within the domestic territory of the United States and also the reinforcements which can be obtained from dependable allies.

The thesis of this book is that a foreign policy consists in bringing into balance, with a comfortable surplus of power in reserve, the nation's commitments and the nation's power. The constant preoccupation of the true statesman is to achieve and maintain this balance. Having determined the foreign commitments which are vitally necessary to his people, he will never rest until he has mustered the force to cover them. In assaying ideals, interests, and ambitions which are to be asserted abroad, his measure of their validity will be the force he can muster at home combined with the support he can find abroad among other nations which have similar ideals, interests, and ambitions.

For nations, as for families, the level may vary at which a solvent balance is struck. If its expenditures are safely within its assured means, a family is solvent when it is poor, or is well-to-do, or is rich. The same principle holds true of nations. The statesman of a strong country may balance its commitments at a high level or at a low. But whether he is conducting the affairs of Germany, which has had dynamic ambitions, or the affairs of Switzerland which seeks only to hold what it already has, or of the United States, he must still bring his ends and means into balance. If he does not, he will follow a course that leads to disaster.

CHAPTER III

THE FOREIGN COMMITMENTS OF THE UNITED STATES

1. The Continental Limits of the United States

WE ARE concerned with the foreign commitments which the American nation is obligated to maintain, if necessary by waging war. These commitments are embodied in laws, as for example the commitment to defend Hawaii or the Panama Canal Zone; in treaties, as in the case of the Philippines or Cuba; in official declarations like the Monroe Doctrine which are held to be binding, and also in conventions, which provide for the defense of the Western Hemisphere.

The primary responsibility for carrying out these foreign commitments rests upon the American people living in continental United States. Thus the defense of Alaska or Hawaii or Luzon or of any other place or any other interest has to be organized and equipped and, for the most part, manned from within continental United States.

Before examining our foreign or external commitments, it will, however, be useful to remind ourselves briefly that most of what is now the American continental homeland was once foreign territory, and that it became United States territory as a result of diplomacy and war.

The War of Independence was won by American arms. But it was not won by American arms alone. In 1778 Benjamin Franklin succeeded in negotiating a treaty of alliance with Vergennes. In this treaty France promised to make common cause with the colonies until they had won their independence, and the colonies promised to defend the French possessions in the West Indies. In 1779 Spain intervened in the war by making New Orleans a base for privateers against British shipping and also by seizing the British posts in West Florida. In 1780 the Netherlands also went to war against Great Britain, and the Czarina of Russia, Catherine II, formed a League of Armed Neutrality which assisted the American colonies by obstructing the use of British sea power.

Thus the American War of Independence was part of a general war in which most of the great powers participated. "So by 1780, the shot at Concord Bridge had literally been heard around the world. There were naval operations on the Atlantic Ocean, the Mediterranean, the Caribbean, the North Sea, the English Channel, even the Indian Ocean." [1] When Cornwallis

[1] Morison, Samuel E., and Henry Steele Commager, *The Growth of the American Republic*, Vol. I, p. 218.

surrendered at Yorktown on October 17, 1781, the British were still firmly in possession of the principal seaports from New York to Savannah. It was by diplomacy that they were ousted. The preliminary Treaty of Peace with England was not signed until November 30, 1782, and it contained the proviso that it was not to take effect until France concluded peace with Great Britain. The Franco-British armistice was not made until January 20, 1783, or the definitive peace until September 3, 1783. This was nearly two years after Yorktown. The reason for the delay was that the American War of Independence, being part of a global war, could not be concluded until a general peace was attained.[2]

The Peace of Paris with the Americans, and the other treaties which England signed on the same day with France and Spain, divided North America among Spain, the British Empire, and the United States.[3] Spain received everything west of the Mississippi and south of a line which gave her Florida. Britain kept what is now Canada, though the boundary was not clearly settled at the time. France took a few West Indian islands.

From this beginning the United States gradually acquired its present continental boundaries in six principal stages from 1803 to 1853.

[2] *Ibid.*, Vol. I, pp. 226–227.
[3] *Ibid.*, p. 228.

First. By the Louisiana Purchase, Jefferson obtained title to New Orleans and the mouth of the Mississippi and to a frontier running through what is now Montana, Wyoming, Colorado, Texas, to Louisiana. This territory between the Mississippi and the Rocky Mountains had been Spanish since 1763. In October 1800, by the secret treaty of San Ildefonso, the King of Spain ceded it to Napoleon. Jefferson was told about the treaty by Rufus King, the United States Minister in London, who heard of it from Lord Hawkesbury.[4] England was then on the point of war with Napoleonic France, and therefore opposed to the aggrandizement of French power in North America. Napoleon in the meantime had met a disaster in Santo Domingo, where thirty-five thousand troops died of yellow fever or were massacred by the Negro insurgents.[5] Assured of support from Britain, Jefferson took advantage of Napoleon's weakness, and through Livingston negotiated with Talleyrand for the purchase of the whole Louisiana territory. The treaty of cession was signed on April 30, 1803.

Second. In 1819, after many border incidents and prolonged negotiation, Spain ceded to the United States all her lands east of the Mississippi,

[4] Clark, J. Reuben, *Memorandum on the Monroe Doctrine*, published by the Department of State, December 17, 1928, p. 22.

[5] Morison and Commager, *op. cit.*, Vol. I., p. 391.

as well as her right to Oregon, in return for the virtual assumption by the United States of its spoliation claims against Spain and the relinquishment of its claims to Texas.

Third. In 1846 President Polk served notice on England that in twelve months the joint occupation of the disputed Oregon territory would end. By negotiations between President Polk and Lord Aberdeen a compromise was reached fixing the present boundaries.

Fourth. In 1846 also, Texas, which had seceded from Mexico, was incorporated into the Union. This territory at that time included most of what is New Mexico, parts of Colorado, Wyoming, Kansas, and Oklahoma.

Fifth. In 1848 at the conclusion of the war with Mexico, the territory which now includes California, Nevada, Arizona, Utah, and part of New Mexico, Colorado, and Wyoming was ceded to the United States.

Sixth. In 1853 the Gila River valley in Southern Arizona and New Mexico was purchased from Mexico under the Gadsden Treaty.

In these six stages the territory of the original thirteen colonies expanded, with minor rectifications, to the present continental limits of the United States. One result was the acquisition of a vast homeland. A second result was, once the independence of the Spanish colonies had been recognized in 1822 and confirmed by the Monroe Doctrine in 1823, the disappearance from North America of France and Spain. After that Britain was the only great power which had a common frontier with the United States. If the boundaries of 1783 had remained the boundaries of the United States, the young Republic would have had to live with France as her neighbor on the Mississippi and with Spain on the frontier of Georgia. This would have left the United States with small means within its narrow limits, and committed to the defense of a long land frontier against the shifting combinations of three great European powers.

The elimination of France in 1803 and of Spain in 1822–1823 left only Britain as a great power in the Western Hemisphere. Upon that foundation of its vastly increased security, the United States opened a new chapter in its history by making a vast *foreign* commitment.

2. *The Western Hemisphere*

This new and different and momentous chapter of our history begins in 1823. In that year the United States assumed an obligation outside of its continental limits. President Monroe extended the protection of the United States to the whole of the Western Hemisphere, and declared that, at the risk of war, the United States would thereafter resist the creation of new European empires in this hemisphere. The prohibition was directed at Spain, France, Russia, and Austria. This momentous engagement was taken by President Monroe, after he had consulted Madison and Jefferson. They approved it only after Canning, the British Foreign Secretary, had assured the American Minister, Richard Rush, that Britain and the British navy would support the United States. For the Founding Fathers understood the realities of foreign policy too well to make commitments without having first made certain they had the means to support them.

They knew, as John Quincy Adams put it, that at that time the naval power of the United States was to that of Great Britain "as a cockboat in the wake of the British man-of-war." [6] The Latin Americans who had revolted from Spain were aware of this, and they looked, says Perkins, "for succor to the mistress of the seas rather than to the young republic of the North. This was true of Bolivar, the Liberator, who wrote in January of 1824 that only England could change the policy of the allies.[7] It was true of Santander, the Vice President of Colombia. It was true of Alaman, the Mexican Foreign Minister. It was true of Rivadavia, the Foreign Minister of Argentina. And when the danger had definitely passed, all of these men recognized that the British attitude had been the really de-

[6] *Memoirs*, VI, p. 179, cited in Dexter Perkins's *Hands Off: a History of the Monroe Doctrine*, p. 43.
[7] I.e. of the Holy Alliance.

cisive one even though they did not ignore the role of the United States. It is, after all, anachronistic in the highest degree to give greater weight to the immature American democracy in 1823 than to the power whose prestige was never greater, whose force was never more impressive, than eight years after the defeat of Napoleon at Waterloo." [8]

Unfortunately, however, for the education of the American people in the realities of foreign policy — that commitments must be balanced by adequate power — the understanding with Britain, which preceded Monroe's Message, was never avowed. To this day most Americans have never heard of it. Yet as a matter of fact the two governments came very near making a joint declaration. On August 20, 1823, Canning, who was the British Foreign Secretary, had proposed to Richard Rush, the American Minister in London, that they sign a convention, or exchange ministerial notes.

Rush held back from the joint declaration because there was a difference in the position of the two countries. The United States had recognized the independence of the Spanish-American nations in 1822, that is to say in the year before the negotiations with England. Canning was not then willing to commit England that far, and would only suggest that she might promise the *future* acknowledgment of the

[8] Perkins, *op. cit.*, p. 68.

South American states.[9] The project of a joint declaration was rejected because the United States was already irrevocably committed, whereas Rush feared that Britain, being uncommitted, might alter her policy and bring it into harmony with that of the Continental powers.[10]

This was in September 1823. Yet in November when President Monroe began the discussion with his Cabinet and with the two ex-Presidents, Jefferson and Madison, he had before him the reports of Rush's negotiations with Canning. In the Cabinet discussions Calhoun, who was Secretary of War, and Southard, who was Secretary of the Navy, wished to give Rush discretionary power to act with Britain. John Quincy Adams, who was Secretary of State, objected that without British recognition of the independence of the South American republics "we can see no foundation upon which the concurrent action of the two governments can be harmonized." [11] He objected to joint action with Britain on the interesting and significant ground that Britain and America, unless both recognized the Spanish republics, would not be "*bound by any permanent community of principle*," and Britain would "still be free to accommodate her policy to any of those distributions of power and partitions of territory which have for the last century been the *ultima ratio* of all European political arrangements."

[9] *Ibid.*, p. 39.   [10] *Ibid.*, p. 38.   [11] *Ibid.*, p. 47.

Adams prevailed, and the American position was stated, not jointly with Britain, but as a unilateral commitment of the United States. But it is clear from Monroe's correspondence with Madison and Jefferson that this bold commitment was made only because the three Virginian Presidents were sure, after studying Rush's report from London, that Britain in her own political and commercial interest would not permit the Holy Alliance (France, Spain, Austria, and Russia) to intervene in South America.

The failure to reach a clear and binding agreement with Britain, based upon a "permanent community of principle," had very serious consequences some years later. In 1858 Napoleon III decided to defy the Monroe Doctrine, and in 1861 sent an invading army into Mexico and established an empire on our southern frontier. He did this at a moment when there was a strong expansionist and annexationist movement in the United States which had led to sympathy with the Mexican revolution. From the point of view of France the time had come to put a stop to the aggrandizement of the American republics and to restore the rights of monarchy in the New World. From the American point of view the success of Napoleon III's venture would have meant the collapse of republicanism in most of this hemisphere and the beginning of a new era of imperialist rivalry.

The American Civil War broke out in April 1861. In October of that year, France induced Great Britain and Spain to agree to joint intervention against the revolutionary government of Juárez. This agreement, reached at a time when the United States was helpless, made it possible for Napoleon to invade Mexico and to enthrone Maximilian as Emperor. In the absence of a permanent binding agreement with the United States, Lord John Russell, who had no liking for the enterprise, nevertheless did not oppose Napoleon, and indeed joined in with him to the extent of sending a few hundred Marines to Mexico. However, soon thereafter Britain withdrew and then tried to persuade Napoleon to desist. Nevertheless, the enterprise went on while the United States was rent by civil war. We might well have had to fight an international war in Mexico as soon as our own Civil War had been concluded. That we did not have to do this was a matter of good luck in that Maximilian was unfortunate in Mexico and Napoleon became involved in troubles at home.[12]

This affair demonstrated how serious was the com-

[12] In this connection it may be pointed out that the other, and perhaps greater, threat to American security in this period was when Lord Palmerston contemplated recognizing the Confederacy. This illustrates another risk of our not having had an avowed alliance with Great Britain.

mitment of the Monroe Doctrine, and how difficult it was to sustain the commitment in the absence of a clear and dependable agreement with Britain. For if Britain had opposed Napoleon at the outset, he could not have ventured into Mexico. If Britain had really supported him effectively, the United States could not have forced him out.

Yet the American people, their minds on other things, never learned the lesson of this experience. Thus they were taught to believe that the immense obligation to protect the Western Hemisphere, and consequently almost any other obligation we chose to assume, could in the nature of things be validated by American forces alone. Because the informal alliance with British sea power was concealed, and was displeasing to their self-esteem, the American people lost the prudence, so consistently practised by the Founding Fathers, of not underestimating the risks of their commitments and of not overestimating their own power.

3. *The Pacific*

With this misunderstanding of the nature of foreign policy, the United States expanded its commitments far beyond the wide limits of the Monroe Doctrine.

In 1844 Caleb Cushing negotiated a treaty with China in which he obtained access to the treaty ports and extraterritorial privileges for American mer-

chants.[13] In 1853 an American naval squadron under
the command of Commodore Matthew C. Perry entered Yado Bay in Japan, and under a mild threat of
force induced the Japanese Shogunate to sign the
Treaty of Kangawa. This act, more than any other,
opened up Japan to foreign intercourse. Mr. Dooley
said of the famous opening of Japan by the American
navy that "we didn't go in; they kim out."

The United States proceeded to expand into the
Pacific. In 1867 Seward bought Alaska from Russia.
Alaska, though part of the North American continent,
was, because of its isolation from the United States
and the lack of land communications, strategically an
island, and therefore it is strategically a foreign commitment. As a measure of the commitment we may
note that the defense of Alaska, and the development
of Alaska as a base of military operations, required
in 1942 an investment of ship tonnage about one third
the size of the tonnage involved in the whole first campaign of the South Pacific or in the first phase of the
North African campaign. As a result of the Alaskan
Purchase the territory of the United States was extended close to Northeastern Asia — to within a few
miles of Russian territory and to within a few hundred
miles of Japan.

In the next two decades the American strategic frontier was extended into the Mid-Pacific. In 1878 a

[13] Morison and Commager, *op. cit.*, Vol. I, p. 612.

coaling station was established at Pago Pago in Samoa. In 1893–1898 the Hawaiian Islands were annexed.[14] By this action the western defenses of the United States were thrust out into a great semicircle from Kiska in the Aleutians through Midway Island to Samoa. From San Francisco as a center the radius of that circle runs over 3000 miles out into the Pacific.

The westward movement continued. During the war with Spain the United States cruiser *Charleston* conquered Guam, in June 1898; and by the Treaty of Paris, made the following December, Spain ceded the Philippine Islands. This committed the United States to the defense of a large territory nearly 5000 nautical miles west of Honolulu and almost 7000 nautical miles west of California, but only 700 miles off the China Coast, only 250 miles from Formosa, only 1700 miles from Yokohama, and less than 1400 miles from Singapore.[15] A circle which has Manila as its center, and a radius of about 1500 miles, encloses the industrial region of Japan, all of Korea, practically all of China proper, French Indo-China, British Burma and Malaya, and the Netherlands Indies. Thus by the acquisition of the Philippines the United States had placed itself at the geographical center of the empires of Eastern Asia, and at the strategic crossroads of their lines of communication.

[14] Midway was acquired in 1859.
[15] A nautical mile = 1.15 statute miles.

This was, as Mahan put it, "a proposition . . . entirely unexpected and novel."[16] It was "Asiatic dominion." The "annexation of the Philippines [was] the widest sweep, in space, of our national extension." A few months after the Senate, by the margin of one vote more than the required two thirds, had ratified the treaty annexing the Philippines, the Secretary of State, John Hay, wrote his notes on the Open Door in China.[17] He followed them by issuing the "circular" of July 3, 1900, which declared that "the policy of the government of the United States is to seek a solution which may" — among other things — "preserve Chinese territorial and administrative entity."

4. At the Turn of the Century

The turn of the century was a critical period in the history of the Republic. For by that time the foreign commitments of the United States, which could be validated in the last analysis only by successful war, had been extended over an immense section of the surface of the globe. On the Atlantic side the line ran approximately from Greenland to the shoulder of Brazil, at about 35° west longitude. On the Pacific side the line was at about 120° east longitude in the Philippines, and even beyond, as the events of 1941 showed, in so far as we were committed to oppose the

[16] Mahan, A. T., *The Problem of Asia*, pp. 7–9.
[17] September 6, 1899.

dismemberment of China. The direct American commitment included the defense of territory from Alaska to Luzon, from Greenland to Brazil, from Canada to the Argentine.

This immense commitment had been made, to be exact, by February 1899. It had been made eighteen years before the United States entered the first World War and some forty-two years before the Japanese attack on Pearl Harbor. No further military commitment of any consequence was made by the United States during the twentieth century. All American military commitments had been made by the end of the nineteenth century. The history of our foreign relations in the twentieth century is a story of failure. It is the story of our national failure to balance the commitments which were made in the nineteenth century. Because of that failure we have been compelled to fight two great unexpected wars for which we were unprepared.

CHAPTER IV

THE BANKRUPTCY OF AMERICAN FOREIGN RELATIONS (1898–1941)

1. President Theodore Roosevelt's Foreign Policy

THE PERIOD of unending domestic controversy over American foreign relations began in January 1899 when the Treaty of Paris, which concluded the war with Spain, was submitted to the Senate for ratification. The debate was held in Executive Session and was unreported.[1] But Senator Henry Cabot Lodge described it as the "closest, hardest fight I have ever known." The opposition to the annexation of the Philippines was led by his colleague, Senator Hoar of Massachusetts. The vote was taken on February 6, 1899, and it was the belief of Theodore Roosevelt that the treaty would have been rejected if the Filipino insurrection, which broke out on February 4, had not been looked upon as a challenge to American prestige. That the outcome was uncertain is clear. A motion to promise the Filipinos ultimate independence was defeated only by the vote of the Vice President,

[1] Griswold, A. Whitney, *The Far Eastern Policy of the U. S.*, pp. 31 *et seq.*

and ratification was obtained by only one vote more than the required two thirds.

The wisdom of the immense commitment to super-impose upon the Monroe Doctrine what Mahan called "Asiatic dominion" was hotly debated not only in the Senate, but in the McKinley-Bryan elections of 1900. It is too late to debate it now. What cannot be gainsaid, however, is that the subsequent foreign policy of the United States has never been equal to the size of the commitment. From the day when Admiral Dewey sailed into Manila Bay until the day when General Wainwright surrendered Corregidor, the United States never made a sustained and prudent, or remotely adequate, effort to bring its obligations and its power into balance.

President Theodore Roosevelt, who, with Senator Lodge and Captain Mahan, was the principal pro-moter of the commitment, did realize that the new departure called for new measures. He saw that we had assumed vast responsibilities in the two oceans. So he insisted upon digging the Panama Canal in order that the navy could be concentrated rapidly in either ocean. He persuaded Congress and the people to sup-port the construction of an enlarged and modern navy.

In his own mind he went further, though he never explained it to the nation or made it a matter of avowed national policy. He knew that in 1900 Germany had staked out her claim to world power by deciding to build a navy so large that it compelled Great Britain "to set about the reduction of her outlying squadrons with a view to mustering her full strength in home waters." [2] He knew that Germany was jealous of the American annexation of the Philippines, and had ordered Admiral von Diederichs to Manila to watch Admiral Dewey. He knew that two days before the battle of Manila Bay, John Hay had sent a telegram from London saying of Germany, "*Voilà l'ennemi* in the present crisis."

Theodore Roosevelt realized that to support our commitments we needed not only the Panama Canal and a strong navy, but also friends and virtual allies — allies against the rising imperialism of Germany, and later on against the rising imperialism of Japan. [3] For that reason President Roosevelt and his Secretary of State, John Hay, never allowed disputes about financial concessions in China to alienate the United States from Great Britain. For the same reason he intervened quickly in the Moroccan Affair of 1905 in order to prevent a European war which, he realized, would leave the United States alone with its vast commitments.

Theodore Roosevelt had, therefore, the elements of a genuine foreign policy. Aware of the American com-

[2] Bywater, Hector C., *Sea-Power in the Pacific*, p. 1.
[3] Japan was not regarded as a strong power until after the Russo-Japanese War of 1905.

mitments, he sought to develop — though tentatively,
unsurely, and without making the matter plain to
the nation — the elements of American power: our
strategic position by constructing the Panama Canal,
our armaments by enlarging the navy, our alliances
by adhering to those powers who were our friends
and the opponents of our opponents. But these rudi-
mentary beginnings of a true foreign policy were not
carried forward by Theodore Roosevelt's successors.

2. *The Persisting Illusion*

In the long period from 1823 to 1898 the nation had
lived in a state of illusory isolation: it was committed
to the Monroe Doctrine, which rested upon the support of British sea power, without having been made
to understand that the defense of the Western Hemisphere did in fact require the support of British sea
power.

The illusion had been confirmed because the Monroe Doctrine had been seriously challenged only by
the Maximilian affair in Mexico, which was easily forgotten. After her defeat by Prussia in 1870 France was
never again capable of entertaining Napoleonic de-
signs. Until about 1900 Germany, though powerful on
land, had no navy with which to threaten the Western
Hemisphere or to reach out into the Pacific. When in
1900 Germany did begin to build a navy, it was obvi-

ous that she would first have to dispose of the British navy before she could look further. Thus for about fifty years after Napoleon III had flagrantly breached the Monroe Doctrine, and had proved that it had been a mistake not to make binding and clear the British support of the commitment, circumstances made it appear falsely that our foreign commitments rested securely upon our geography, our inherent virtues, and our own isolated military strength.

Successive generations of Americans lived, therefore, in the illusion that our position and our commitments were inviolable. The mental habits of Theodore Roosevelt's immediate successors — Taft and Wilson — were formed in that period of illusory isolation which had lasted from 1823 to 1898. Both were idealists who habitually rejected the premises of the politics of power. Both disliked armaments. In them the idealism which prompts Americans to make large and resounding commitments was combined with the pacifism which causes Americans to shrink from the measures of force that are needed to support the commitments. Neither promoted the preparation of armaments in time of peace. Both accepted reluctantly and tardily the need to arm. Both abhorred as inherently vicious and unnecessary, and as contrary to American principles, the formation of alliances. But both favored a League of Nations in which the United States assumed the obligation to enforce peace.

Thus the seeds of a genuine foreign policy, which Theodore Roosevelt planted, never matured. A national understanding of what is a foreign policy was never inculcated into the minds of the later American generations. When the long-expected war in Europe broke out in 1914, the United States had no foreign policy which enabled the nation to determine its interests in the conflict. President Wilson had no foreign policy, accepted by the nation, which gave him the means of judging whether, why, when, where, how, and to what end, the United States must take its position in the war.

From 1914 to 1916 Wilson vacillated between the assertion of American rights and reluctance to face the consequences of asserting them, between dread of a German victory and dread of a war to prevent a German victory. Thus he took a zigzag course, now one way because the British blockade infringed the American doctrine of the freedom of the seas, now the other way because German ruthlessness outraged American sensibilities. Lacking a foreign policy, and with leaders whose training was wholly in domestic politics, the nation had no means of ascertaining its true interests. The verbal battle of the propagandists, of which so much was made in later years, was fought in this vacuum of the American mind. It was fought because the American nation lacked even the rudiments of a settled foreign policy which could make clear whose victory and what kind of victory would best serve the vital interests of the United States.

Because of this vacuum, the United States went to war in April 1917 for reasons which were never willingly or accurately avowed. And so they were never clearly recognized.

3. President Wilson's Foreign Policy

The occasion for going to war was Germany's unrestricted use of the submarine against American merchant shipping on the Atlantic routes from North America to the British Isles and France. But the substantial and compelling reason for going to war was that the cutting of the Atlantic communications meant the starvation of Britain and, therefore, the conquest of Western Europe by imperial Germany.

President Wilson avoided this explanation of his decision to intervene, choosing instead to base his decision upon the specific legal objection to unrestricted submarine warfare and upon a generalized moral objection to lawless and cruel aggression. But these superficial reasons for the declaration of war would never have carried the day if a majority of the people had not recognized intuitively, and if some Americans had not seen clearly,[4] what the threatened German

[4] Cf. "The Defense of the Atlantic World," an editorial in the *New Republic*, February 17, 1917 (Vol. X, No. 120). [When I wrote this article I had the oppor-

victory would mean to the United States. Though there was lacking the tradition of a foreign policy which made the matter self-evident, many Americans saw in 1917 that if Germany won, the United States would have to face a new and aggressively expanding German empire which had made Britain, France, and Russia its vassals, and Japan its ally. They saw that in such a position the defense of the Western Hemi-

---

tunity to know what Colonel House and others among Wilson's advisers were thinking. — W. L.]

". . . It means that our fundamental interest in this crisis is not a complicated system of rights but a definite and practical and tangible end. The world's highway shall not be closed to the western Allies if America has power to prevent it.

"We do not hesitate to say that this should be American policy even though submarines were capable of successful, humane 'cruiser warfare.' We do not hesitate to say — we have believed it and said it since the beginning of the war — that if the Allied fleet were in danger of destruction, if Germany had a chance of securing command of the seas, our navy ought to be joined to the British in order to prevent it. The safety of the Atlantic highway is something for which America should fight.

"Why? Because on the two shores of the Atlantic Ocean there has grown up a profound web of interest which joins together the western world. Britain, France, Italy, even Spain, Belgium, Holland, the Scandinavian nations, and Pan-America are in the main one community in their deepest needs and their deepest purposes. They have a common interest in the ocean which unites them. They are today more inextricably bound together than sphere would require immense armaments over and above those needed in the Pacific, and that America would have to live in a perpetual state of high and alert military preparedness. It was in this very concrete and practical sense, though unhappily President Wilson preferred not to particularize, that a German victory in 1917 would have made the world unsafe

---

most even as yet realize. But if that community were destroyed we should know what we had lost. We should understand then the meaning of the unfortified Canadian frontier, of the common protection given Latin America by the British and American fleets.

"It is the crime of Germany that she is trying to make hideous the highways by which the Atlantic Powers live. That is what has raised us against her in this war. Had she stood on the defensive against France and Britain, had she limited the war to the Balkans and the eastern front where it originated, and thrown in her lot with the western nations, she would have had their neutrality and probably their sympathy. But when she carried the war to the Atlantic by violating Belgium, by invading France, by striking against Britain, and by attempting to disrupt us, neutrality of spirit or action was out of the question. And now that she is seeking to cut the vital highways of our world we can no longer stand by. We cannot betray the Atlantic community by submitting. If not civilization, at least our civilization is at stake.

"A victory on the high seas would be a triumph of that class which aims to make Germany the leader of the East against the West, the leader ultimately of a German-Russian-Japanese coalition against the Atlantic world. . . ."

for the American democracies from Canada to the Argentine.

This in brief was the undeclared, and only partially realized, foreign policy which determined the participation of the United States in the first German World War. The sinking of merchant ships without visit and search, and without provision for the safety of crews and passengers, would not in itself have been the *casus belli* if the German submarines had caused less destruction. Sporadic sinkings would have continued to lead to protests, as they did in 1915 and 1916, and probably to reprisals. But they would not have led to war if by 1917 the submarine had not become so destructive as to make it seem probable that Germany would starve out Britain and isolate France.

Nor did the United States go to war to make the world safe for all democracies: [5] if it had seemed probable that Germany would be defeated by Czarist Russia, the United States would have remained neutral because its vital interests in the North Atlantic would have remained secure. The war was certainly not engaged to overthrow the Kaiser and to make Germany a democratic republic: if the Germans had not broken into the Atlantic and threatened the whole structure

[5] I am using the Wilsonian phrase "safe for democracy" in the popularly accepted sense of the words, though, as I have tried to indicate, I believe this is an erroneous interpretation of their substantial meaning.

of our Atlantic defenses, private citizens would still have made faces at the Kaiser, but the nation would not have made war upon him.

The United States did not go to war because it wished to found a League of Nations; it went to war in order to preserve American security. And when the war was over, the nation would almost certainly have accepted in some form or other the scheme of the League of Nations if President Wilson had been able to demonstrate to the people that the League would perpetuate the security which the military victory had won for them. Mr. Wilson failed to make this demonstration. He failed because in leading the nation to war he had failed to give the durable and compelling reasons for the momentous decision. The reasons he did give were legalistic and moralistic and idealistic reasons, rather than the substantial and vital reason that the security of the United States demanded that no aggressively expanding imperial power, like Germany, should be allowed to gain the mastery of the Atlantic Ocean.

Because this simple and self-evident American interest was not candidly made explicit, the nation never understood clearly why it had entered the war. As time went on, the country was, therefore, open to every suggestion and insinuation that the nation had fought for no good reason at all, that its victory was meaningless, that it had been maneuvered into a non-

American war by the international bankers and the British diplomats. And so, having failed to make plain that the war was waged for a vital American interest, President Wilson had no way of proving to the nation that his settlement of the war really concerned the United States. The war had been fought without a foreign policy, and neither President Wilson nor the nation had the means, therefore, of judging whether the League was merely a foreign or was also an American interest.

Thus the longer the Senate debated the Treaty of Versailles with its covenant, the more the people felt that there was no compelling connection between their vital interests and the program which President Wilson offered them. They saw that the League imposed upon the United States the unprecedented commitment to help enforce the peace of Europe. They saw only what they were asked to contribute. For they had not been taught to understand what British and French power meant to the security of America's vital interests all over the world.

They had not had it demonstrated to them how much the defense of the Western Hemisphere depended upon having friendly and strong partners in the British Isles, in the French ports on the Atlantic, at Gibraltar and Casablanca and Dakar; or how much the defense of the Philippines depended upon French Indo-China, and upon British Hong Kong, Malaya, and Burma, and upon the attitude and the strength of

Russia and upon China in Eastern Asia. The legalistic, moralistic, idealistic presentation of the war and of the League obscured the realities — caused it to appear that for what we were asked to give to our allies, we were to receive nothing from them. It was made to seem that the new responsibilities of the League flowed from President Wilson's philanthropy and not from the vital necessity of finding allies to support America's vast existing commitments in the Western Hemisphere and all the way across the Pacific to the China Coast.

Not until twenty years later, not until France had fallen and Britain was in mortal peril, not until the Japanese had surrounded the Philippines, did it become possible for the nation to perceive the hidden but real structure of America's strategic position in the world.

4. The Collapse of U. S. Foreign Policy

As I have tried to show, the nation had no foreign policy to guide it during the historic half century in which the United States has waged three wars. President McKinley, who made the momentous commitment in the Philippines, asked at first only for the island of Luzon, then for the whole archipelago, and also for one island in the Ladrones, which turned out to be Guam. But in 1899 he let Spain sell the rest of the Ladrones and the Marianas and the Carolines to Germany.

These islands which are the barrier between the Philippines and Hawaii were seized by Japan in 1914. At the Peace Conference in Paris, President Wilson agreed to let Japan retain them under a theoretical and unenforceable mandate from the League of Nations. From these islands the attack on Pearl Harbor was launched. Because Japan held these islands it was impossible to reinforce General MacArthur. Such a neglect of American interest, such a failure to see the value of these islands, would have been impossible if Americans had had the habit of maintaining a foreign policy. The Japanese, who had a foreign policy, even if it was a pernicious policy, knew why they wanted the strategic islands. We, who had no foreign policy, did not know enough to care about the islands.

Still larger consequences flowed from our national failure to develop a foreign policy. After the rejection of Wilson's settlement, American foreign relations were conducted for twenty years without any indication that the nation had any conception of its commitments. In 1922 we reduced our naval strength to a ratio which gave Japan naval superiority in the Western Pacific. We agreed also not to improve the fortifications of Corregidor, Cavite, and Guam, which lay under the guns of the Japanese fleet. At the same time we renewed our commitment to oppose Japanese imperialism in Asia and to encourage Chinese resistance to it. Thus at the very time when we were reducing our power we renewed and even enlarged our commitments.

Knowing that Japan was the only possible enemy we had to consider in the Pacific, we nevertheless turned upon our natural partners, Britain and France, and treated them as rivals whose armaments it was a diplomatic triumph to reduce. Though we observed scrupulously our own promise not to fortify Guam or to reinforce the defenses of the Philippines, we submitted to the Japanese refusal to let us know what she was doing in her islands. But the more we disarmed ourselves and our natural allies in the coming Pacific war, the more vehemently we committed ourselves to oppose Japanese expansion.

The climax of this unbelievably reckless conduct was reached in the summer of 1939, two months before the outbreak of the second German World War. In July of that summer a majority of the Senate Committee on Foreign Relations took two decisions. One was to advise the State Department to declare economic war against Japan by abrogating the Commercial Treaty.[6] The treaty was abrogated and Japan was put on notice that we were her avowed antagonists. The Committee's second decision was to refuse to lift the arms embargo which prevented Britain and France from buying arms here to resist Germany —

[6] S. Res. 166, July 18, 1939.

the Germany which had been allied with Japan since 1936!

It would be hard to find a more perfect example of total incompetence in guiding the foreign relations of a people. The Senate Committee invited a war in the Pacific while it deliberately refused to take measures to fortify our ancient defenses in the Atlantic. This monstrous imprudence was what passed for American foreign policy at the outbreak of the present war.

5. President Franklin D. Roosevelt's Pre-war Position

It was then that the emasculation of American foreign policy reached its extreme limit — the limit of total absurdity and total bankruptcy. The events of the perilous thirties, which were inaugurated by the Japanese conquest of Manchuria and the rise of Hitler, had led inexorably to a world war waged from Europe and from Asia against our vital interests and our inescapable commitments. At this juncture we found ourselves opposed to our future enemies but with our exposed possessions undefended, without allies, isolated from our friends, and yet committed over the length of the Western Hemisphere and across the vast expanse of the Pacific. At the zenith of our commitments we were at the nadir of our precautions.

Eventually there is a reckoning for nations, as for individuals, who have obligations that are not covered by their resources. Between 1931 and 1937 it had become manifest that the time of that reckoning had come. Japan's seizure of Manchuria had proved that the collective opinion of mankind, which all our statesmen loved to invoke, was no deterrent to the aggressor. The Italian conquest of Abyssinia in 1935, the successful intervention of Germany and Italy in Spain, the rearmament of Germany, the reoccupation of the Rhineland, the Anti-Comintern Pact which in fact allied Germany with Japan, and the invasion of China proper in 1937 — these events made it unmistakably clear that Germany and Japan and Italy were on the march and that they would dominate the world if they were not successfully resisted.

From 1937, when he made his "quarantine" speech in Chicago until the Japanese attack on Pearl Harbor, President Roosevelt struggled with the problem of making our bankrupt foreign position solvent. As early as 1937 it was clear that the American situation demanded an immediate, intensified expansion of our armed forces, the fortification of our strategic commitments in Alaska, Guam, the Philippines, and Panama, and the formation of arrangements for mutual aid with Great Britain, France, and China — our obvious allies in an attack which was being prepared against them and against us alike. But this prudent course was held to be politically imprudent. This is another way of saying that the American people would not agree to protect their vital interests because they had no foreign policy which disclosed their vital interests.

Thus from 1937 to 1940 President Roosevelt moved anxiously and hesitantly between his knowledge of what ought to be done and his estimate of how much the people would understand what ought to be done. I shall not attempt to answer the question whether he could have made the people understand how great was their peril because their commitments were totally unbalanced. The illusions of a century stood in the way of their understanding, and it may be that no words, but only the awful experience of total war, could even partially dispel the illusion.

In any event the fact is that Mr. Roosevelt did not succeed in persuading the nation to attend effectively to the American interest. Though he understood it himself, though he realized the peril, in action he followed events, taking small measures to repair great disasters which were undermining the American position in all the strategic areas of the world. Thus he did not insist on greater armaments until after the Japanese had conquered the coast of China, had encircled the Philippines, and were poised for the attack on Singapore, Burma, and the Netherlands Indies. Not until after France had fallen and had left exposed the bulge of Africa, where it juts out against the bulge of Brazil, not until Britain was threatened with invasion and her fleet with destruction or capture, did he feel able to move at all.

He did not feel able to do what was needed because of the series of furious controversies which divided the nation between 1937 and 1941 — over the repeal of the arms embargo, over the transaction of the over-age destroyers and the bases, over conscription, over lend-lease, and over the repeal of the Neutrality Act. None of these costly controversies would have taken the form it did take if the President had been able to present it to a people which realized how serious were their commitments and had acquired the habit of covering their commitments.

Thus almost none of the so-called isolationists declared that the commitments of the United States should be reduced — that the Monroe Doctrine should be revoked, that the Philippines should not be defended, that Japan should be given the free hand in China which she demanded as the price of peace. The isolationist party adhered, on the whole, to our vast trans-oceanic commitments. They devoted their efforts to opposing the alliances which, as is now obvious, we needed in order to validate the commitments. They argued that only by doing nothing to save our present allies from defeat would we be able to stay out of war. This was the ground on which they opposed the repeal of the arms embargo, the transfer of the destroyers, and lend-lease. They took this view because they felt confident that continental United States could not be invaded, and they chose to ignore as a disagreeable anomaly the fact that American obligations extended to South America and to islands 7000 miles west of the coast of California. Isolationism, in other words, was based on a failure to appreciate the long-established trans-oceanic commitments of the United States.

The case of the "interventionists" rested on a correct appreciation of the situation — that alone and without allies the United States could not sustain its commitments against the combined power of the totalitarian alliance. Yet not until only the British Isles and the armies of General Chiang Kai-shek were left did the President feel it expedient in domestic politics to avow openly this self-evident truth. Even then it was still regarded as the Roosevelt policy rather than as the American national policy.

And even now, as we approach the climax of the struggle, it is still by no means certain that a settled American policy can be established against the abiding illusions of more than a century of inexperience in the realities of foreign policy.

CHAPTER V

MIRAGES

THE HABITS of a century have fostered prejudices and illusions that vitiate our capacity to think effectively about foreign relations. The elementary means by which all foreign policy must be conducted are the armed forces of the nation, the arrangement of its strategic position, and the choice of its alliances. In the American ideology of our times these things had come to be regarded as militaristic, imperialistic, reactionary, and archaic; the proper concern of right-minded men was held to be peace, disarmament, and a choice between non-intervention and collective security.

We not only ignored the development of the means to achieve our ends: we chose as the ends of our efforts a set of ideals which were incompatible with all the means of achieving any ideals. The ideal of peace diverted our attention from the idea of national security. The ideal of disarmament caused us to be inadequately armed. The apparently opposed ideals of non-intervention on the one hand, and of collective security on the other, had at bottom the same practical result in that they inhibited us from forming our necessary alliances. Thus for nearly half a century after our vast commitments in the Pacific had been superimposed upon our immense commitment in the Western Hemisphere, we have had to conduct our pre-war diplomacy verbally — by promises, threats, and exhortations;[1] we have had to wage war three times without being prepared to fight; and we have twice made peace without knowing what we wanted.

These spendthrift habits have led us to the bankruptcy of a total war in which we have suffered humiliating initial disasters at the hands of the Japanese; and our very independence was for a time in jeopardy. The habits of mind of Americans of our generation are quite alien to those of the Founders of the Republic. Washington, Hamilton, Jefferson, Madison, Monroe, entertained none of the basic illusions and prejudices which have dominated the later generations of Americans. They did not regard peace as more important than the national security. Though Jefferson had some odd ideas about the navy, the Founders never thought of making unpreparedness for war a national ideal. And though they spoke against "entangling" alliances, they never hesitated to seek the support of other powers, as in the case of the Louisiana

[1] Cf. (1) Wilson's notes to the belligerents, 1914–1916; (2) Kellogg-Briand Pact, 1928; (3) *Peace and War: U. S. Foreign Policy 1931–1941.*

Purchase and the declaration of the Monroe Doctrine, when they saw that directly or indirectly the help of an ally could promote the national interest.

The idealistic objections to preparedness, to strategic precautions, and to alliances came to dominate American thinking in the hundred years which followed Monroe's declaration. The objections flourished, and became a national ideology, owing to the historical accident that in that period Asia was dormant, Europe divided, and Britain's command of the sea unchallenged. As a result, we never had to meet our obligations in this hemisphere and in the Pacific, and we enjoyed a security which in fact we took almost no measures to sustain.

This unearned security during a long century had the effect upon our national habits of mind which the lazy enjoyment of unearned income so often has upon the descendants of a hard-working grandfather. It caused us to forget that man has to earn his security and his liberty as he has to earn his living. We came to think that our privileged position was a natural right, and then to believe that our unearned security was the reward of our moral superiority. Finally we came to argue, like the idle rich who regard work as something for menials, that a concern with the foundations of national security, with arms, with strategy, and with diplomacy, was beneath our dignity as idealists.

1. "Peace"

So we must examine our national prejudices, and we may begin by asking ourselves whether peace, as so many say, is the supreme end of foreign policy. Merely to ask the question would have sounded shocking a short while ago. At the moment, it is obvious that the survival of the nation in its independence and its security is a greater end than peace. For we can see now that a surrender to Japan and Germany would give us peace, and the more absolute the surrender, the more absolute the peace. If the American people laid down their arms forever and agreed to obey without resisting any demand of their present enemies, the United States would have peace with its enemies. If the other United Nations could be persuaded to surrender also, the only remaining danger of war would be in being drafted, like the Vichy French or the Slovaks or the Siamese, in the event of war between Japan and Germany for the ultimate mastery of the globe.

If the logic of peace as the supreme national ideal leads to absurdity, then it must be a grave error to think and to say that peace is the supreme end. For national ideals should not express amiable but unconsidered sentiments. They should express the serious purposes of the nation, and the vice of the pacifist ideal is that it conceals the true end of foreign policy. The true end is to provide for the security of the nation in peace *and* in war. This means that, as far as human foresight and prudence can make it so, the vital interests of the nation must be so legitimate that the people will think them worth defending at the risk of war — and that they must be safeguarded so that they can be defended successfully in case of war. A nation has security when it does not have to sacrifice its legitimate interests to avoid war and is able, if challenged, to maintain them by war.

This has always been the view of statesmen who understood their responsibilities. It is, I submit, what Washington meant when he said in the Farewell Address that *"we may choose peace or war*, as our interest, guided by justice, shall counsel." Washington did not say that the nation should or could renounce war, and seek only peace. For he knew that the national "interest, guided by justice" might bring the Republic into conflict with other nations. Since he knew that the conflict might be irreconcilable by negotiation and compromise, his primary concern was to make sure that the national interest was wisely and adequately supported by armaments, suitable frontiers, and the appropriate alliances.[2]

[2] Contrary to the widespread impression, Washington believed in alliances, provided they were appropriate to the existing needs. Had he not welcomed the alliance with France? Cf. Chapter V, section 3.

The untoward result of the pacifist ideal is to cause the nation to neglect its defenses and to ignore its enemies. For national policy, we must never forget, controls at the most only national action: thus the pacifist nation can disarm itself but it does not disarm its enemies. This quandary is not resolved by saying that if all nations could be persuaded by argument or example to adopt the pacifist ideal, there would be no more wars and no further need to be prepared for war. This is the error of acting today on the assumption that you have already achieved what you dimly hope you may be able to achieve tomorrow. For until all the nation's rivals and potential enemies are irrevocably committed to the pacifist ideal, it is a form of criminal negligence to act as if they were already committed to it.

The course of events from the seizure of Manchuria in 1931 to the invasion of Poland in 1939 has proved how the pacifist ideal in Great Britain, France, and the United States permitted and even encouraged the ambitions of the aggressive states. The example of the British, who were sincerely opposed to war, and of the Americans who had their neutrality law, did not persuade our present enemies. It merely caused them to think that they would not meet the resistance of the British and the Americans. Then, when at last they were resisted, their memory of the pacifist utterances caused them to complain bitterly that they

had been cheated of an easy conquest by a conspiracy of hypocrites.

Thus the preachment and the practice of pacifists
in Britain and America were a cause of the World
War. They were the cause of the failure to keep
pace with the growth of German and Japanese armaments.[3] They led to the policy of so-called appeasement, which is merely a general name for that sense of
impotence which caused the Allies to surrender strategic assets, like Czechoslovakia and Indo-China, that
the enemy needed in order to mount his great offen-
sives. The surrender of the Rhineland in 1936, and
that of Austria and Czechoslovakia in 1938, were the
strategic preliminaries to the neutralization of Russia
and the conquest of Poland in 1939. What was surrendered by our allies in the name of peace became
the strategic foundation upon which Hitler prosecuted
his war.

We may call this the vicious circle of pacifism. In
the name of peace the nation is made weak and un-
willing to defend its vital interests. Confronted with
the menace of superior force, it then surrenders its
vital interests. The pacifist statesmen justify their
surrender on the ground, first, that peace is always
preferable to war, and second, that because the nation

[3] Cf. collected speeches of Winston Churchill, 1932–
1938, published in the United States under the title *While
England Slept.*

wants peace so much, it is not prepared to wage war. Finally, with its back to the wall, the pacifist nation has to fight nevertheless. But then it fights against a strategically superior enemy; it fights with its own armaments insufficient and with its alliances shattered. This was the way in which the pacifist ideal led the peace-loving nations to the very edge of the catastrophe from which they are now saving themselves only at prodigious cost. The generation which most sincerely and elaborately declared that peace is the supreme end of foreign policy got not peace, but a most devastating war.

2. *"Disarmament"*

In the interval between the two great wars the United States sought to promote peace by denouncing war, even by "outlawing" it, and by disarming itself, Great Britain, and France. The movement to limit armaments was, no doubt, inspired in considerable measure by sheer war-weariness and by the desire to save money. But the disinterested and idealistic theory of disarmament was that if everyone had less capacity to wage war, there would be a smaller likelihood of war. Big warships meant big wars. Smaller warships meant smaller wars. No warships might eventually mean no wars. The theory is applicable, if at all, only to Tibet, which has no foreign relations, cannot be invaded, is not worth conquering, and has no outlying commitments such as the Monroe Doctrine, the Philippines, and Alaska.

Yet on the theory that disarmament could promote peace, laborious negotiations and elaborate diplomacy and splendid international conferences were promoted in Washington, Geneva, and London. The governments participating were the victorious allies of the first German World War. It soon transpired that though the promise of these conferences was that smaller armaments would banish war, the working premise of all the governments was that each of the former allies was now the rival, and therefore the potential enemy, of all the others. The disarmament movement was, as the event has shown, tragically successful in disarming the nations that believed in disarmament. The net effect was to dissolve the alliance among the victors of the first World War, and to reduce them to almost disastrous impotence on the eve of the second World War.

The movement for peace by disarmament was initiated by President Harding, who summoned our ex-allies to the Washington Conference. In the light of its consequences, the American program at that conference is interesting. We insisted upon the rupture of the Anglo-Japanese alliance, thus isolating Japan and offering her the option of finding new allies among the vanquished states. Japan made her new alliance with Germany. We then committed ourselves and the other powers to the moral support of the territorial integrity of China, aligning ourselves against the known ambitions of Japan. We then "imposed," as we imagined, a ratio of naval forces, especially of the long-range offensive ships, which guaranteed Japan against any prompt and effective naval intervention by America or Britain in the Far Eastern area of Japanese ambition. We then gave Japan hostages to reinsure herself. We did this by agreeing not to develop our advanced naval bases at Guam and Manila. Then, inspired by a peaceable desire not to annoy the Japanese, we assented by our subsequent silence and inaction to the militarization of the mandated islands which protected Japan's flank in her march to the conquest of the Philippines and of the Indies. Finally, having disarmed ourselves strategically vis-à-vis Japan, we worked with the British on the project of reducing the tactical value of their navy and of ours,[4] and upon arresting for twenty years the progress of the art of naval construction in Britain and in America.

The overall effect has been to impair radically the Anglo-American control of the sea communications of the world. That was not the intention, of course. It was supposed that if the ratio of the fleets was maintained, the balance of power would be the same, though the fleets were smaller. This was a fallacy in

[4] Cf. the prolonged controversy about cruiser types.

calculation. For, as the absolute size of the British and American fleets was reduced, the area in which they could operate contracted. The British did not have enough ships to maintain an effective fleet at Singapore. They were not sure of having enough ships to control the Mediterranean. We did not have enough ships to maintain our communications in the Atlantic. In the first year of the present war we did not even have enough ships to defend our coastal traffic and the waters of the Caribbean. The reduced British fleet had to be concentrated at the British Isles. The reduced American fleet had to be concentrated between California and Hawaii. Thus Japan obtained superiority in all the waters that mattered to her, and Britain's sea power was so depleted in the Mediterranean that even Italy dared to challenge her.

The story of the disarmament movement is the sorry tale of nations which lost sight of their own vital interests, and very nearly emasculated themselves fatally as a result. For more than a hundred years the marriage, in Jefferson's metaphor, of British and American sea power had supported the Monroe Doctrine. The American people did not know it, and, lacking the elementary principles of a foreign policy, they did not wish to hear about it. Though Britain and America had been allies in 1917–1918, yet in the twenty years which elapsed before they became allies again they acted as if they were potential enemies.

This assumption controlled the disarmament movement — that extraordinary movement by which the partners of one great war disarmed one another in the short period which remained before they were to be partners again in an even greater war.

3. *"No Entangling Alliances"*

The hard core of resistance to the formation of foreign policy has been the popular objection to alliances. For over a century Americans have believed that the undesirability of alliances was so self-evident as to be outside the pale of discussion. Now an objection which men will not examine and debate is a prejudice. This prejudice rests, so most of us were brought up to believe, upon the teachings of the Founding Fathers of the Republic.

Yet as a matter of fact the Founding Fathers did not hold the prejudice against alliances which latter-day Americans have ascribed to them. The record of their words and their acts shows that whenever they thought it would serve the national interest to have the support of allies, they were only too pleased to have allies. In the War of Independence Washington rejoiced when Franklin succeeded with Vergennes in making an ally of the King of France, and Americans did not disdain the support of Holland and of Russia. In the great affair of the Louisiana Purchase, by means of which the Mississippi Valley became

American territory, Jefferson did not shrink from ac-
cepting the diplomatic encouragement of Britain. And
finally, in the last great act in foreign relations which
was determined by the Founding Fathers of the Republic, in the preparation of the Monroe Doctrine,
they made their decision after negotiations in London
by which they were assured of the armed diplomatic
support of Great Britain. Far from sharing the popular
prejudice against alliances, they made alliances, at one
time and another, with France and Britain, the two
greatest foreign powers of their time.

How then did we come to think that alliances were
contrary to the example of the Founding Fathers, and
therefore alien to the purest American tradition? I
believe that the reason is simple. For seventy-five
years after the adoption of the Monroe Doctrine, the
unavowed but none the less actual British-American
community of interest which supported it worked on
the whole so well that, as with the air we breathe or
our stomachs when they are in good order, we were
unconscious of the implied alliance. Thus American
historians and American statesmen lacked the incen-
tive to make clear the true history of the foreign
policy of the Founding Fathers, and a few passages,
torn from their context and then misread, were treated
as the Holy Writ of American tradition.

These phrases come from Washington's Farewell
Address (September 17, 1796) and from Jefferson's

First Inaugural (March 4, 1801). The passage from Washington states that "Europe has a set of primary interests which to us have none or a very remote relation," and therefore "it must be unwise in us to implicate ourselves by artificial ties in the ordinary vicissitudes of her politics or the ordinary combinations and collisions of her friendships or enmities." When these words were written in 1796 the French Revolution and its subsequent wars were fiercely dividing the ideological sympathies of the people of the young Republic between the supporters of England and of France. We may measure the bitterness of the division by the fact that in a private letter written at the time, Jefferson, whose sympathies were then with France, referred to Washington as a "Samson in the field and Solomon in the Council" whose head had been "shorn by the harlot England." [5] This was the kind of thing which Washington had in mind when he warned the nation against the ideologies and the foreign propagandists, against the "excessive partiality for one foreign nation and excessive dislike of another" which may "cause those whom they actuate to see danger only on one side, and serve to veil and even second the arts of influence on the other."

Not wishing to be drawn into the European War on the side of France against England, he then went on

[5] Quoted in Morison and Commager, *op. cit.*, Vol. I, p. 369.

to argue that the alliance made with France in 1778, which played such a decisive part in the War of Independence, should not be regarded as a *permanent* alliance to support France in all her wars. "It is our true policy," he said, "to steer clear of permanent alliances with any portion of the foreign world, so far, I mean, as we are now at liberty to do it; for let me not be understood as capable of patronizing infidelity to existing engagements." What he objected to was extending the French alliance to include the obligation to help France in Europe: "I repeat, therefore, let those engagements [with France] be observed in their genuine sense. But in my opinion it is *unnecessary and would be unwise to extend them.*" These are not the words of a man with a dogmatic prejudice against all alliances as such: these are the words of a man cautiously measuring the necessity and wisdom of extending an alliance.

Evidently, Washington, who had helped to send Franklin and others to the European capitals to obtain their support in an American war, was not the man to propose dogmatically that America would never need allies and must never form alliances. He concluded the celebrated passage on foreign policy by saying that "taking care always to keep ourselves by suitable establishments on respectable defensive posture, we may safely trust to temporary alliances for extraordinary emergencies." Two years later Washington accepted the command, with the rank of Lieutenant General, of an American army which was raised to make war against France, and if that new war had come, if Talleyrand had not yielded, Washington would have fought as an ally of Great Britain.

Surely it is clear that while Washington was opposed to permanent alliances which would involve the United States in the disputes *within Europe,* he took it for granted that where American interests were at stake, temporary alliances with European powers were desirable.[6] How could the comrade in arms of Lafayette and De Grasse have been the opponent of all alliances as such?

He was, it is true, opposed to "permanent alliances." But in studying Washington's advice, we have to remember that when he spoke in 1796 the United States had only a commitment to defend the French West Indian colonies under the treaty of alliance of 1778. Washington did not regard this commitment, which lapsed a few years later, as permanent. It was only thirty years later that the United States made a foreign commitment, in fact a permanent foreign commitment which covered the whole of the Western Hemisphere. Perhaps Washington would have opposed the commitment. But if he had agreed to it, can we in justice to him be sure that he would have made a permanent commitment of such gravity without making certain

[6] Cf. Chapter X.

that the only effective way of making it good was no less permanently assured?

The acts of his immediate successors must, we may reasonably assume, throw light upon these questions.

The celebrated injunction to seek "honest friendship with all nations, entangling alliances with none" comes from Jefferson's First Inaugural. It is no less clear that Jefferson, like Washington, had no dogmatic prejudice against alliances as such. For, where an American interest, as he conceived it, was at stake, he sought as a matter of course for the appropriate ally. On April 18, 1802, thirteen months after uttering the words about entangling alliances, we find President Jefferson writing to Robert R. Livingston, the American Minister in Paris, about the cession of Louisiana by Spain to France: Jefferson, who had always been strongly pro-French, writes that though we have looked on France as "our natural friend," there "is on the globe one single spot the possessor of which is our natural and habitual enemy." That spot is New Orleans, which controls the mouth of the Mississippi. "The day that France takes possession of New Orleans . . . seals the union of two nations, who, in conjunction, can maintain exclusive possession of the ocean. From that moment, we must marry ourselves to the British fleet and nation. We must turn all our attention to a maritime force, for which our resources place us on very high ground; and having formed and

connected together a power which may render rein-
forcement of her settlements here impossible to France,
make the first cannon which shall be fired in Europe
the signal for the tearing up of any settlement she
may have made, and for holding the two continents of
America in sequestration for the common purposes of
the United British and American nations." [7]

Jefferson's conviction that the defense of American
interests in the Western Hemisphere was closely related to an alliance with British seapower stayed with
him to the end of his days. It survived the War of
1812 with England. In 1823 when Spain, France,
Austria, and Russia were threatening to intervene in
the Americas, President Monroe, as we have already
seen, consulted Jefferson about making the commitment of the Monroe Doctrine. He sent Jefferson the
record of the Canning-Rush negotiations, and then
analyzed the problem as follows: —

> 1st, Shall we entangle ourselves, at all, in
> European politicks, & wars, on the side of any
> power, against others, presuming that a concert
> by agreement,[8] of the kind proposed, may lead
> to that result?

[7] President Jefferson's "United British and American
nations" is an interesting forerunner of President Roosevelt's phrase "United Nations," invented by him during
a visit of Prime Minister Churchill at the White House.
[8] With Britain.

2nd, If a case can exist, in which a sound maxim may & ought to be departed from, is not the present instance, precisely that case?

3rd, Has not the epoch arrived when Great Britain must take her stand, either on the side of the Monarchs of Europe, or of the United States, & in consequence, either in favor of Despotism or of liberty, & may it not be presumed, that aware of that necessity, her government has seized on the present occurrence, as that, which it seems the most suitable, to announce & mark the commencement of that career? [9]

Jefferson replied to the President that "the question presented by the letters you have sent me is the most momentous which has ever been offered to my contemplation since that of independence. That made us a nation, *this sets our compass and points the course* which we are to steer through the ocean of time opening on us." And what was the course to which the author of the injunction against entangling alliances advised the President to commit the nation? He advised the President to make what Monroe had called "a concert by agreement" with Great Britain, saying "Great Britain is the nation which can do us the most harm of any one, or all on earth; and with her on our side we need not fear the whole world . . . with Great Britain withdrawn from their scale" — that is of

[9] Clark, *op. cit.*, p. 97.

the European powers — "and shifted into that of our two continents, all Europe combined would not undertake such a war" — as the Holy Alliance was threatening — "for how would they propose to get at either enemy" — Britain or America — "without superior fleets?"

Madison, who was also consulted by President Monroe, took the same view. A week before the Cabinet decided in favor of the great commitment he wrote to President Monroe that "with the British power and navy combined with our own, we have nothing to fear from the rest of the world; and in the great struggle of the epoch between liberty and despotism, we owe it to ourselves to sustain the former, in this hemisphere at least. I have even suggested an invitation to the British government to join in applying the 'small effort for so much good' to the French invasion of Spain, and to make Greece an object of some such favorable attention."

As we know, President Monroe made the concert with Great Britain — not "by agreement" but by implicit reliance upon the common interest. Yet in effect it was an alliance though it was unavowed publicly and never formally ratified. The understanding reached by Rush and Canning endured for long. On the whole it worked satisfactorily. The concert of the two nations in the Western Hemisphere, and in the defense of their vital interests, lasted for nearly a century and a quarter. As early as 1802 Jefferson had already seen the probable need for it.

Thus we are entitled to say that the objection of latter-day Americans to alliances is not based on the authority of the Founders of the Republic. It rests on an obscuration of the words, the acts, and the explicit beliefs of Washington, Jefferson, Madison, and Monroe. We may add that the concert by agreement, which in 1823 three of the early Presidents united in taking as the premise of their greatest commitment, was so successful that later generations thought the beneficent results were due to the nature of things — for example, to the width of the ocean — and not to an act of the highest statesmanship. The work of art was so good for so long that the artists who labored to produce it were forgotten. The Anglo-American concert conferred such enormous benefits in keeping two continents free of imperialism and of war, and for so long exacted no payment in return, that in our times men have refused to recognize, because events did not compel them to recognize, that the effective substance of an alliance with Britain was the cardinal element in American foreign relations.

For seventy-five years Monroe's concert with Great Britain provided adequate force to cover the foreign commitments of the United States. After 1899, when the Senate had ratified the treaty of peace with Spain, the structure of policy built by Jefferson, Madison, and Monroe was no longer adequate. They had dealt with the commitment to protect the Western Hemisphere; after 1899 American commitments had been extended across the Pacific to the China Coast. As the liabilities increased, the assets on the other side of the balance sheet decreased. For three quarters of a century after Monroe made his concert, Great Britain was the undisputed mistress of the seven seas. But in 1900 Germany, already a great land power, began to build a great navy, and soon thereafter Japan followed suit.

The older Germany had, as Bismarck said in 1871, held that "it is far from our purpose to get a footing anywhere in America, and we recognize in relation to the whole continent the predominant influence of the United States as founded in the nature of things, and compatible with our interests." [10] But by 1902–1903 the German view had changed to such a degree that the Foreign Office was not allowed by Admiral von Tirpitz and others to renew publicly Bismarck's acceptance of the Monroe Doctrine.[11] Germany's challenge to British sea power coincided with Germany's growing challenge to the hemispheric position of the United States.

Thus the old order of our foreign relations, as it had persisted from 1823, was radically dislocated after

[10] Perkins, *op. cit.*, p. 150.
[11] *Idem.*, p. 223.

1900. Our commitments had been extended to Asia
and the Anglo-American concert was challenged by
the new German navy and the new German imperialism.

At this historic turning point the nation needed
great new increments of military force and an extension of its political agreements. They were needed
in order to cover the new Asiatic commitment. And
they were needed to reinsure the United States against
the German threat to British sea power in the Atlantic.
Monroe's concert of implied but not avowed and binding agreement was no longer sufficient. For it covered
only the Atlantic; it assumed that Britain's command
of the sea was invincible. There was no agreement with
any supporting power in the Pacific though the United
States had obligations on the other side of the Pacific.

Yet American statesmanship, lacking the clarity of
Monroe, Jefferson, and Madison, was no longer equal
to the task of estimating commitments and power, liabilities and assets, risks and precautions. For forty
years after the old order of American foreign relations
had ceased to exist, the American nation clung to the
illusions which had sufficed under the old order. The
adherence to this old and now obsolete policy is known
as "isolationism." The name is misleading. In reality
our commitments had been greatly extended, whereas
our power and that of Britain had relatively dimin-
ished. The correct name for the policy of keeping the

commitments without enlarging our power and our alliances is not isolationism, but insolvency.

During the forty years in which the practice of insolvency prevailed, most Americans would have said that, despite the strength of the pacifist movement for disarmament, they believed in "adequate national defense." But the prejudice against alliances was so deep and so stubborn that in our foreign relations we refused to distinguish between those nations whose vital interests made them our potential allies and those nations whose opposing interests made them potential foes. Thus we were as zealous in seeking to disarm Britain as Japan, and from 1914 to 1916, and again from September 1939 to June 1940, American policy professed to see no vital American interest in whether Britain or Germany won the war.

The prejudice against alliances obliterated the essential distinction between friend and foe. Unable to say who was friend and who was foe, who our ally and who our enemy, we had no practical measure of what was meant by the words "adequate national defense." Adequate against whom? Adequate with the help of whom? The word "adequate" had no meaning, and thus the real measure of our military preparation was not what would be needed to win a probable war but what Congress, belabored by the pacifists, militarists, the domestic pressure groups, and the taxpayers, agreed to appropriate money for.

4. "*Collective Security*"

When the prejudice against alliances encountered the desire to abolish war, the result was the Wilsonian conception of collective security. As Wilson saw it, the cause of the first World War was the system of alliances which had divided Europe into the Triple Alliance and the Triple Entente, and in his mind it was necessary to liquidate alliances in order to organize peace through the League of Nations. Articles 23, 24, 25, were written into the Covenant by President Wilson in order to liquidate old alliances and prevent the formation of new ones. Thus collective security was to be the remedy and the substitute for alliances.

There was a negligible minority at the time who did not share this, the Wilsonian view, but held that a system of collective security could not be maintained unless within it there existed an alliance of strong and dependable powers.[12] They held that a nucleus

[12] Cf. e.g. Walter Lippmann *The Political Scene. An Essay on the Victory of 1918*, pp. 41–42. "An Anglo-American entente means the substitution of a pool for a balance, and in that pool will be found the ultimate force upon which rests the League of Nations. For if the united power of Britain and America — potential and actual — is wielded for the ends they now both officially profess, they are assured of the active assistance of the smaller nations everywhere. The reason for this is that they exercise a form of force — sea power — which is irresistible in conflict and yet cannot be used permanently to conscript

of leading states, allied for the defense of their vital interests, was needed in order to enforce peace through a system of collective security.

Wilson, however, not only shared the traditional prejudices against alliances but was deeply influenced also by the idea that the nations could be brought together by consent, as the thirteen American colonies had been brought together first in a confederation and then in a federal union. This analogy has long been cherished by Americans as affording the hope that it might become a model for the rest of the world.

Yet it is, I submit, a profoundly misleading analogy. For the thirteen colonies had been planted and had matured under one sovereign power, that of the English crown. They had fought the War of Independence under the government of a Continental Congress which resolved to draw up Articles of Confederation even before the Battle of Bunker Hill, which adopted the Articles in 1777, and saw them ratified and in force before Cornwallis surrendered at Yorktown. The former colonies remained a confederation after the war

and enslave alien peoples. Nor does it rest internally upon the existence of a large caste in control of a regimented population. Sea power can be all-powerful without destroying the liberties of the nation which exercises it, and only free peoples can be trusted with great power. In spite of the comparison between navalism and militarism there are these fundamental differences between them, and they are appreciated by the bulk of the world."

was over, and when they adopted the present Constitution they were, as they themselves insisted, forming "a more perfect union."

They were not forming an altogether unprecedented union, they were perpetuating and perfecting a union which had always existed since the plantation of the British colonies. The fact that none of the Spanish or French colonies joined the union is fairly conclusive evidence that even in North America — three thousand miles from Europe — political unions do not become more comprehensive by voluntary consent.

If the historic experience of Britain, France, Russia, Germany, and Italy is a guide, it tells us that the large states have grown up around the nucleus of a strong principality — England, the Île de France, Muscovy, Piedmont, Prussia. By conquest, by royal marriages, by providing protection to weaker principalities, by the gravitation of the smaller to the bigger, the large national unions were gradually pulled together.

President Wilson's conception of collective security did not take into account this historic pattern. He held that there should be a union of fifty juridically equal but otherwise unequal states, and not the evolution of a union from a nucleus of firmly allied strong states. Refusing to regard alliances as the effective means by which collective security could be made to operate, Wilson forbade the founders of the League of Nations to perfect their alliance which had been tested in the fires of war. He did, to be sure, reluctantly agree to the French demand for a special guarantee in return for France's giving up the Rhine frontier. But he regarded this as a compromise of his principles and readily abandoned it.

Wilson identified collective security with antipathy to alliances, rather than with the constructive development of alliances. The influence of this idea played a great part in dividing the Americans from the British and the French, and the British from the French. For the French saw from the first, being closer to the realities of Europe, that the League could enforce the peace only if the League were led by a strong combination of powers resolved to enforce the peace. The French, therefore, sought allies in Europe, all the more urgently as they saw their alliance with Britain dissolving. This alienated the British, who believed in the Wilsonian League, and pushed them toward encouraging the German revolt against the settlement.

Then, as time went on, the League became impotent because the nuclear alliance of Britain, France, and America had been dissolved. Above all, the League was impotent to prevent our present enemies from forming their Tripartite Pact. Twenty years after the League was founded, the great military alliance of Germany, Italy, and Japan had been formed. But the generalized, abstract system of collective security had fallen to pieces.

It will be said that the Wilsonian ideal could have been realized if the Senate had not refused to ratify the Treaty of Versailles. Perhaps so. But if it had been realized, the League would, I submit, have succeeded, because American participation would in practice have been tantamount to a working nuclear alliance — in Monroe's phrase to "a concert by agreement" — with Great Britain primarily, and with France indirectly. This alliance has had to be reconstructed in order to conduct the present war. If it had existed after 1919, and had been perfected, it might have prevented the present war. Certainly it would at least have prevented Britain and America from disarming one another in the presence of Japan and Germany. And if the war had come nevertheless, we should not have been brought so perilously near to disaster.

The American opponents of the League saw truly that if the League was actually going to enforce peace, then it must imply the equivalent of an Anglo-American alliance. If the League did not imply that, then the generalized commitments of the Covenant were too broad and too unpredictable to be intelligible. Thus Wilson was placed in a dilemma: if the League was a practical instrument, it contained an alliance, and all good and true men including Wilson were opposed to any idea of an alliance; if in fact the League outlawed alliances, and still sought to enforce peace, then it was an unlimited commitment supported by no clear means of fulfilling it. Thus the League was attacked both as a concealed alliance in the realm of power politics and as a utopian pipe dream.

The dilemma was presented because Wilson was trying to establish collective security without forming an alliance. He wanted the omelet. He rejected the idea of cooking the eggs. The people, agreeing that an alliance was abhorrent, proceeded by intuitive common sense to the conviction that without an alliance, the League was unworkable and unpredictably dangerous.

Thus in the debacle of Wilson's proposals we see the culminating effect of the American misunderstanding of alliances. Wilson as well as the men who opposed him had carried over into the twentieth century the illusion fostered in the nineteenth century — that the United States had never had allies and that the purest American tradition was opposed to alliances. The concert with Britain, which Monroe, Jefferson, and Madison had established in 1823, had been the foundation of American foreign relations for seventy-five years. But though it existed in fact, it had never been avowed as a policy.

Thus in the fateful period from 1898 to 1941 the United States engaged in three wars but never succeeded in forming a foreign policy. We could have had a foreign policy only by agreeing that since our commitments had been extended, a concert by agreement had to be extended correspondingly. But the modes of thought which Washington, Jefferson, and Madison had as a matter of course used had been forgotten through disuse. Thus the nation was unable to form any foreign policy after the war with Spain, or after the first World War. And as yet it has not been able to form a policy in the second World War.

PART TWO

CHAPTER VI

THE STRUCTURE OF THE AMERICAN POSITION

1. A Parenthesis on Foreign Policy and Domestic Dissension

WE COME now to the object of our inquiry. It is to discover and elucidate the valid foreign policy of the United States in our own time. The acid test of our success must be whether our positive conclusions point to the common ground upon which the American people, who have been deeply divided on foreign policy for nearly fifty years, can again unite. This is the test, though there are many, I know, who would say that the people must be persuaded to unite in order to permit their statesmen to form a sound foreign policy. But I am arguing that before the nation can be united, a sound foreign policy has to be discovered and formulated.

The reader will, I hope, agree that this test — that those who have disagreed are brought toward agreement — is a correct and necessary measure of a valid foreign policy. Our experience since the foundation of the Republic has shown that domestic division over

foreign relations is the outward and visible consequence — and not the cause — of an insolvent foreign
policy. Thus the first thirty years — from 1789 to
1823 — were a period of deep dissension, so deep that
the burden of Washington's Farewell Address is his
foreboding that factionalism in regard to foreign affairs
would destroy the Republic. It did not do that. But it
might have done that. In the troubled period of the
Napoleonic era the young Republic was so torn within
that the New England states were threatening to secede
from the union. The internal dissension which em-
bittered the first twenty years of the Republic re-
flected an unclarified and unsettled foreign policy.
This policy was erratic to the point of bringing the
United States to the verge of war with France and
later into actual war with England, and finally face
to face with the menacing prospect of armed intervention in this hemisphere by the combined great
powers of continental Europe.

This troubled period came to an end only in 1823
with the adoption by Monroe, Jefferson, and Madison
of the concert with Great Britain. By that act of
statesmanship the foreign policy of the United States
became solvent — its foreign commitments were in
accord with its vital interests and the means to sustain
the commitments were more than adequate. Then, and
then only, did foreign relations cease to be great
domestic issues: with respect to the strong powers of

the world, American relations were firmly settled. Disputes with other nations beyond our borders were disposed of by diplomacy or by localized war, like the Mexican, in which the vital security of the nation was not at stake, in which the risks and the consequences were limited.

The solvent period in American relations lasted for about seventy-five years — from the establishment of the Monroe Doctrine until the treaty of peace under which Spain ceded the Philippine Islands. In this solvent period it was predominantly true, except in the case of the Mexican War, which did not involve our relations with great powers, that foreign affairs were not a serious domestic issue. But since 1899 American foreign relations have never, as we have seen in the first part of this book, been solvent. Accordingly, the nation has been deeply divided throughout this period. It has been divided on the issues of imperialism, on intervention in the first World War, on participation in the settlement of that war, on reconstruction after that war, on measures to prevent the second World War, on preparedness for it, on intervention in it, and on what course to take when it ends.

Insolvency, then, is the cause of the dissension. In the affairs of a corporation or of a state a fiscal position which points to bankruptcy will cause demoralizing dissension about income and expenditures, about taxes, debts, and appropriations. These dissensions cannot end until the fiscal position has been reorganized by a budget which, because it is balanced, re-establishes the common measure to which the disputants submit. In the foreign relations of a nation the items on the two sides of the ledger cannot be reduced to the common denominator of the dollar. The items on both sides of the account include incommensurables and intangibles. Nevertheless there is a grim accounting if the budget of foreign relations is insolvent. The accounting is in war. Insolvency in foreign policy will mean that preventable wars are not prevented, that unavoidable wars are fought without being adequately prepared for them, and that settlements are made which are the prelude to a new cycle of unprevented wars, unprepared wars, and unworkable settlements.

During this grim cycle the people will be strongly divided among themselves by reason of the fact that their foreign relations are insolvent. We have been living in this grim cycle for nearly fifty years. The cycle can be broken now only as it was broken after the troubled period in the early days of the Republic: by the formulation of a policy which, because it is sound, works so well that it heals the dissension.

The example of Monroe, Jefferson, and Madison teaches us that while a true policy will win the assent of the people, the policy will not be formulated if the responsible statesmen shirk the responsibility of making the initial decision. Monroe announced to Congress the policy which he and Madison and Jefferson had decided upon. He did what he conceived to be right and necessary. The correspondence of the three Virginia Presidents is concerned not with what the Gallup poll might show about the opinions of the people, but with what the vital interests of the country required in the situation as it presented itself. They did not ask whether the people, who were divided, could be induced to support a sound policy. They formulated a sound policy which the divided people came, because of its inherent virtue, to unite in supporting. This was that leadership by statesmen without which democracy is nothing but the vain attempt of men to lift themselves by their own bootstraps.

In our age, to be sure, a great policy cannot be adopted, as it was in 1823, by private consultation among a few leading men. But the essential principle is not changed: the measure of a policy is its soundness; if it is sound, it will prove acceptable. The policy must be examined on its merits and not with respect to its immediate popularity. Here we take our stand on the fundamental proposition that in their foreign relations the people have in fact a common interest, and that if we have the wit to discern it correctly, and the patience to elucidate it cogently, the true policy which emerges will unite the common sense of the nation because it is self-evident, and indeed commonplace.

The policy which is signified by the Monroe Doctrine became an American commonplace, and that is what a sound policy must be. For upon the effects of foreign policy are staked the lives, the fortunes, and the honor of the people, and a free people cannot and should not be asked to fight and bleed, to work and sweat, for ends which they do not hold to be so compelling that they are self-evident.

With these preliminary observations we may begin our effort to define the American foreign policy which is suitable to the present age.

2. *The Defensive Area of the United States*

When we speak of the "vital interests of the nation" we mean those interests which the people of the nation are agreed they must defend at the risk of their lives. Even those who, like Gandhi, believe in the doctrine of non-violence do not put the preservation of their own lives above the defense of what they hold to be the vital interest of the community. They are prepared to die in a hunger strike or to be crushed by the advancing Juggernaut, rather than to yield. Though they differ from most men as to the weapons they will employ and the causes for which they are prepared to die, they recognize that there are vital interests which transcend their own lives. Thus they too are a force in human affairs. Only those who would not defend any interest are inert to a point where they have no part in human affairs.

No demonstration is needed, of course, that the American nation will fight for what it regards as its vital interests. The internal disputes have turned upon the question: What are the vital interests of the United States?

Thus there was very considerable opposition to Jefferson's purchase of the Louisiana territory, and the constitutionality of the act was not upheld by the Supreme Court until twenty-five years later.[1] We find it difficult to realize today that American patriots ever thought that the Mississippi Valley was not a vital American interest. The war with Mexico (1846), which turned on the annexation of Texas and California, was opposed by the Whigs.[2] The Massachusetts Legislature declared that it was a war of conquest, a war to strengthen the slave power, a war against the free states, and unconstitutional. James Russell Lowell wrote in the *Biglow Papers:* —

> They may talk o' Freedom's airy
>   Tell they're pupple in the face;
> It's a grand gret cemetary
>   Fer the barthrights of our race;
> They just want this Californy
>   So's to lug new slave-states in,
> To abuse ye, an' to scorn ye,
>   An' to plunder ye like sin.

[1] In *American Insurance Co.* v. *Canter* 1828. Cf. Morison and Commager, *op. cit.*, Vol. I, p. 392.

[2] *Ibid.*, pp. 591–593.

As a member of Congress, Abraham Lincoln defended the vote of his party,[3] "declaring that the war with Mexico was unnecessarily and unconstitutionally commenced by the President [Polk]." He accused the President, as Sandburg tells us, of "marching an American army out of proven American territory into land not established as American soil."

But once the continental homeland had become *proven American territory*, its defense as against foreign powers became a universally recognized vital interest. This was accomplished between Yorktown and Appomattox. Since 1865 the continental limits of the United States have been stabilized at the Canadian and Mexican boundaries, and between the Atlantic and the Pacific.

But these continental limits have never corresponded with the defensive frontiers of the United States. This is evident when we remember that the French invasion of Mexico in 1861 was regarded by Americans as a hostile act, and that any threat against Canada would be so regarded as a matter of course. Until as recently as 1940 we have had no formal defensive alliance with Canada, or until 1941 with Mexico.[4] But the sub-

[3] January 12, 1848. Cf. Sandburg, Carl, *The Prairie Years*, Vol. I, p. 367.

[4] The date of the Ogdensburg Agreement was August 18, 1940, and the date of the Mexican-American Agreement was November 19, 1941.

stance of these alliances has long existed — in the case of Canada since the Treaty of Ghent (1814), and with Mexico since the affair of Maximilian (1861–1867).

The lands which the American nation was prepared to defend in war have since 1823 included the whole of the Western Hemisphere. It is a fact that the Monroe Doctrine has not always been rigidly enforced. The challenge of Napoleon III found the United States unable to respond immediately. Although this threat was liquidated without war, we nevertheless indicated our intention by mobilizing the United States army. Andrew Jackson did not dispute the British annexation of the Falkland Islands in 1833 or the founding of the British establishments at Belize in what had been Guatemalan territory. Perhaps he knew how much the Monroe Doctrine depended upon "the concert" with Great Britain which Rush and Canning had negotiated, which Monroe, Jefferson, and Madison had approved. Jackson might reasonably have felt that the anomalies were more apparent than real. For only Britain, which for generations provided the principal military support of the Doctrine against all the rest of Europe, has been allowed to improve her strategic position in this hemisphere — the case of the Falkland Islands — and to make a small breach of the general principle — the case of British Honduras.[5] Thus, despite

[5] In regard to the controversy with Great Britain during Cleveland's administration over arbitration of

a long series of diplomatic disputes, it is true that the tentative defensive frontiers as laid down and conceived by Monroe have more and more become the accepted frontiers upon which the American nation would fight.

Unfriendly foreign critics of the Monroe Doctrine

---

the boundary between Venezuela and British Guiana, cf. Allan Nevins, *Grover Cleveland*, Chapter XXXIV; Dexter Perkins, *Hands Off*, *A History of the Monroe Doctrine*, pp. 171–191; Olney's note, Lord Salisbury's reply, and Cleveland's messages in *Foreign Relations of the United States*, 1895, Part I.

The territory had been in dispute since Britain took over her part of Guiana from the Dutch in 1814. The question was dormant until 1886. Then Venezuela broke off diplomatic relations with Britain after the British, following a refusal of Venezuela to compromise, had proclaimed their line as the boundary. Cleveland insisted on arbitration. There was an exchange of notes between Olney and Salisbury in which both statesmen lost their tempers and said what they had better not have said. Olney, for example, declared that "today the United States is practically sovereign on this continent and its fiat is law upon the subjects to which it confines its interposition. Why? . . . because . . . its infinite resources combined with its isolated position render it master of the situation and practically invulnerable as against any or all other powers." When Olney wrote these words the United States had one modern battleship. Salisbury replied by saying that the Venezuela-Guiana boundary dispute had nothing to do with the Monroe Doctrine in that the question was "simply the determination of the frontier of a British possession have called it the cloak of United States imperialism. Domestic critics have occasionally argued that the commitment was too extensive, and that it should be contracted to the line of the Amazon River and the bulge of Brazil. The question whether the defense of the whole of South America against invasion or intrusion by a non-American power is a vital interest of

---

which belonged to the Throne of England long before the Republic of Venezuela came into existence" and that the "United States is not entitled to affirm as a universal proposition, with reference to a number of independent states for whose conduct it assumes no responsibility, that its interests are necessarily concerned in whatever may befall those states simply because they are situated in the Western Hemisphere."

The excitement ran high for a brief period. But on both sides of the Atlantic, sober opinion soon prevailed. In 1896 Arthur Balfour declared in a speech at Manchester that the time must come when some statesmen of greater authority even than Monroe "will lay down the doctrine that between English-speaking peoples war is impossible." Britain yielded and agreed to arbitration. Cleveland appointed a commission headed by Associate Justice Brewer, and the arbitral tribunal "upheld the principal British contentions, but at two points it gave Venezuela territory within the Schomburgk line." (Nevins, *op. cit.*, p. 647.) In 1898, Olney, who had twisted the lion's tail in his note of July 20, 1895, made a speech saying that "the two peoples . . . take with each other liberties of speech which only the fondest and dearest relatives indulge in. Nevertheless, they will be found standing together against any alien foe by whom either was menaced by destruction or irreparable calamity."

the United States was raised as late as 1940.[6] The answer to that question clarifies our understanding of what is a vital national interest. The American people saw in 1940 that if we acquiesced in the establishment of the military power of Germany or Japan in the region south of the Amazon, we should be confronted with a direct and continual menace to the security of the regions north of the Amazon. The three Virginia Presidents had seen that clearly more than a century before. With the spectacular development of the striking force of air power, it was even more evident in 1940. The presence of hostile land-based air power in South America, and the command of sea and air communications from Europe and Africa across the South Atlantic to South America, would have placed the United States permanently and dangerously on the defensive.

Thus the true defensive region of the security of the United States is the land mass of North and South America. This is the region which has to be defended against invasion, intrusion, and absorption by conspiracy within; and if lost, it would have to be liberated.

3. *The Failure of the Passive Defense*

During the nineteenth century British sea power had unchallenged command of the approaches to the

[6] Cf. e.g. address by General Robert E. Wood before Chicago Council on Foreign Relations, October 4, 1940.

Americas. In that era it was, therefore, possible for the United States to assume that Britain would provide the primary strategic defense by restraining the trans-oceanic powers, and that ours was the secondary obligation of defending the territories of the two Americas. Yet this strategic doctrine was valid only as long as no superior combination of hostile trans-oceanic powers was able to come into being.

As soon, then, as Britain no longer ruled all the oceans — which was after about 1900 — our own strategic doctrine ceased to be adequate. The immense coast line of the two Americas cannot be defended by standing guard on the beaches and by manning the coastal defenses, or even by a navy based upon the Americas and, therefore, compelled to let the enemy decide where and when he would strike.

The immense risk of the static defense had already been demonstrated in the war with Spain. Mahan pointed out in his *Lessons of the War with Spain* that Admiral Cervera left the Cape Verde Islands on April 29, 1898, and no one knew where he was until he touched at Martinique on May 11. That was the first news of Cervera's whereabouts that reached Admiral Sampson, who had part of the United States fleet at Puerto Rico, and Admiral Schley, who had the other part of it at Hampton Roads. Thus Cervera reached Santiago on the nineteenth of May while Sampson reached Havana on the twenty-first and Schley reached Cienfuegos on the twenty-second.

"We cannot," said Mahan, "expect ever again to have an enemy so entirely inapt as Spain showed herself to be; yet, even so, Cervera's division reached Santiago . . . two days before our divisions appeared in the full strength they could muster before Havana and Cienfuegos." [7]

Cervera was unable to do in Cuban waters what the Japanese, some forty years later, did at Pearl Harbor — namely, strike a telling blow before his whereabouts were discovered. But he might have done that. The United States fleet was divided between Puerto Rico and Hampton Roads because it was bound by the doctrine of the static defense of the home territory; Cervera, who was weaker than the two American fleets combined, might with luck and more skill have destroyed the separated parts.

It follows that the American regions cannot be defended by waiting to repel an attack initiated by a formidable enemy. Therefore, the strategic defenses of the United States are not at the three-mile limit in American waters, but extend across both oceans and to all the trans-oceanic lands from which an attack by sea or by air can be launched. American security at sea has always, as Monroe, Jefferson, and Madison saw so clearly, extended to the coast line of Europe,

[7] Mahan, Alfred T., *Lessons of the War with Spain* (1899), p. 157 — from *Mahan on Naval Warfare* edited by Allan Westcott, p. 241.

Africa, and Asia.[8] In the new age of air power it extends beyond the coast line to the lands where there are airdromes from which planes can take off.

4. *The Naked Elements of the U. S. Position*

This enables us to state the fundamental conception upon which the foreign policy of the United States must be formed.

Between the New World and the Old there is an ocean of sea and air.

The two Americas are, in relation to the rest of the world, islands in this ocean.

They are also islands in respect to one another. For the Isthmus of Panama is not an effective land bridge.

Moreover, the greater part of the inhabited portion of South America, below the bulge of Brazil, is at present more easily accessible by sea, and in some respects by air, to and from Europe and Africa than it is to and from the arsenals and military depots of the United States.

At the same time North America is more accessible to and from the British Isles, Western Europe, Russia, and Japan than it is accessible to and from South America, or China, or the South Pacific.

[8] Monroe's Message is no less concerned with the Russian advance down the Pacific Coast from Asia than with the threat of the Quadruple Alliance in Europe against South and Central America.

Thus, among the great powers, the nearest neighbors of the United States are Britain, Russia, and Japan. They are also, with the exception of Germany, the principal military powers of the modern world — that is to say the powers which are most capable in the present era of raising large fighting forces and of arming them with the most modern weapons.

The relations of Britain, Russia, Japan, and the United States — as foes, as allies, or as neutrals — has since about 1900 regulated, and will for the predictable future regulate, the issues of peace and war for the New World. Germany, the other principal military power, bears upon the New World as the enemy or as the ally of the other great powers who are our nearer neighbors. Thus in the first World War it was no longer possible for the United States to be neutral towards Germany when in 1917 she threatened, by conquering Britain, to become our nearest neighbor. In the second World War, neutrality became impossible when in 1940 Germany, which was already the ally of Japan, was again threatening to become our nearest neighbor by conquering Britain. *Our* vital relations with Germany depend upon *her* relations with Britain, Russia, and Japan.

This is the system of power within which the United States is living. It is necessary to fix clearly in view these naked elements of our position in the world. For otherwise it is not likely that we can form a foreign policy in which we define lucidly our true interests, recognize the meaning of our commitments and the means of fulfilling them.

The defense of South America is, for example, a vital interest of the United States. But since South America contains no principal military power which can help greatly to insure the defense, we must — as Monroe, Jefferson, and Madison realized — regard the defense of South America as a heavy commitment. It is a commitment which can be challenged only by one of the great powers of the Northern Hemisphere, and the fulfillment of our commitment depends upon whether, in our relations with the great powers, our friends outweigh our foes.

Our other relations are also controlled by the alignment of the great powers within the system. Thus it is theoretically possible for the United States alone to fulfill its obligation in the Philippines, or even its moral obligation to insure the integrity of China. But even theoretically an isolated victory over Japan is possible only if the United States is not engaged in a great war elsewhere and if Japan has no effective ally in her war with us. In fact, as the event has shown, a separate and isolated Japanese-American War is an impossibility. The course of war between Japan and the United States is regulated by the relationship among all the great powers.

The fact of the matter is that the principal military

powers form a system in which they must all be at peace or all at war. This is not a new and recent development in human affairs brought about by the rapidity of modern communications. It has been the condition of American life since the European settlement of the New World. It is nothing but an illusion, fostered by the false reading of history, which has led so many to think that America has ever been able to stay out of any great war in which there was at stake the order of power in the oceans which surround the Americas. The people who live on this continent have from the beginning of their history been involved in the relations of war and peace among the great powers which face the same ocean.

The settlement in North America by men who spoke English and read the English Bible and adhered to the English common law did not begin until more than a century after the voyages of Columbus. The settlement began in fact in the generation which followed the triumph of British over Spanish sea power in 1588. Before that change in the order of power there was already a great Spanish Empire extending from Florida to Peru. But there were no English settlements until the Northern Atlantic ocean highway had been opened to the colonists who planted themselves in Virginia and in Massachusetts Bay. Beginning in 1688 and ending in 1815 a series of great wars was fought between Britain and France. In all of them Americans participated, sometimes with the

British and sometimes against them. They fought with the British in what Europeans call the War of the League of Augsburg (1688–1697), the War of the Spanish Succession (1701–1714), the War of the Austrian Succession (1740–1748), the Seven Years' War (1756–1763). The American phases of these wars are called King William's War, Queen Anne's War, King George's War, the French and Indian Wars. To be sure the Americans fought in these wars as colonists owing allegiance to the British crown. But that does not alter the fact that in the great wars in Europe there were at stake American affairs. Nor does it alter the fact that in severing the British connection the Americans sought allies in Europe, nor the fact that after the British connection had been severed Americans were immediately involved in all the great wars within the order of power. During the Napoleonic Era they waged the Quasi-War against France, and the War of 1812 against England. They formed the concert with Britain to resist the Holy Alliance. They have fought in both the German wars of the twentieth century.

There have been no other great wars which involved the order of power in our surrounding oceans. The Crimean, the Franco-Prussian, the Sino-Japanese, the Russo-Japanese, and the Balkan Wars did not, at the time they were fought, affect the order of power in which America moves. The supremacy of British sea power and Monroe's concert with it were not at issue in these wars, and from these wars America could and did remain aloof.

Therefore, though the nations which have played a leading part in the order of power have changed in the course of three centuries, there has never been a time when the vital interests of America were not involved in that order. It has been merely an accident that for more than a hundred years after Monroe the order of power was so stable that Americans forgot that it existed. And in spite of our two great wars of the twentieth century it is still uncertain whether the nation has learned to appreciate the reality of its position among the great powers.

Yet it is not possible to be prepared for war or to make a lasting peace unless the nation is able to form a foreign policy based upon its true position in the order of power.

5. *The Order of Power*

The fundamental subject of foreign policy is how a nation stands in relation to the principal military powers. For only the great powers can wage great wars. Only a great power can resist a great power. Only a great power can defeat a great power. And therefore the relationship of his nation with the other great powers is the paramount — not by any means the sole, but the paramount — concern of the maker of foreign policy. Unless this relationship is such that the combination against him is not stronger than the combination to which he belongs, his foreign policy is not solvent: his commitments exceed his means, and he is leading his people into grave trouble.

Therefore, no great power can be indifferent to any of the other great powers. It must take a position in regard to all of them. No great power can stand alone against all the others. For none can be great enough for that. If its object is to win a war it has chosen to wage, or not to lose a war imposed upon it, a great power must have allies among the great powers. And if its object is, as ours must be, to preserve the peace, then it must form a combination of indisputably preponderant power with other great states which also desire peace.

Thus the statesman, who means to maintain peace, can no more ignore the order of power than an engineer can ignore the mechanics of physical force. He should not, to be sure, frivolously "play power politics." But he must with cold calculation organize and regulate the politics of power. If he does not do that, and do it correctly, the result must be a cycle of disastrous wars followed by peace settlements which breed more wars.

For a hundred years between Waterloo and the invasion of Belgium there existed in the world an order of power which was good enough to prevent a great war. There were localized, limited, short wars, but there was no general and total war. Over this order Great Britain presided by means of her unchallenged command of the seas. Within this order Germany, Japan, and the United States developed into great powers. But this order of the nineteenth century was unique in modern history and the very fact that it favored the rise of new powers meant that the order was certain to be transitional.

By the turn of the century the old order no longer corresponded with the true distribution of power in the world, and — since men were not wise enough and good enough to construct a new order of power — there began the cycle of twentieth-century wars. During this period none of the great states has been able to form a workable foreign policy. One and all they have misjudged the forces with them and the forces against them, and until they construct an order of power which fits the realities of power, they must continue in the cycle of disaster.

In 1914 Germany, with no ally except the rapidly decomposing former great power, Austria-Hungary, went to war with a combination of great powers which finally included all the great powers. This insured her defeat. Germany realized her error, and in 1939 she thought she had corrected it. She had made alliances with Italy and Japan, two of her former enemies, and a pact with a third, Russia; and she carefully cultivated the isolationism of the fourth, America. Thus she inaugurated her second war under auspicious circumstances, and won rapid, spectacular, and cheap victories. But then she fell into the error she had sought to avoid. Instead of wooing the vanquished, she infuriated them. Instead of placating the neutrals, she menaced them: Russia by invading her, America by threatening South America and by promoting the alliance with Japan. This brought into being the great coalition which will destroy Germany's power.

The foreign policy of Japan during this same period consisted in antagonizing all her neighbors — Russia, China, Britain, the Netherlands, and the United States. The only ally she made was Germany, which was not a Far Eastern power. Therefore, the Japanese policy was a sheer gamble on the hope that Germany would engage all the great powers so as to give her a free hand. The gamble was correct in the year 1942. But only for that year. For Japan had risked everything to win everything in a war which, as regards the final alignment of power, was being decided on the other side of the world.

The foreign policy of the other states was in this period no less misguided and very nearly as disastrous. At the armistice of 1918 they constituted a combination so strong that they had within their reach the means to construct a new order of power. But they did not do this. On the contrary they dissolved the combination. First, they ostracized Russia, being more concerned with the passing danger of an ideology than with the permanent order of power. Then they isolated Japan. Then they isolated themselves one from the other — America from Britain, and Britain from France, and France from Italy. When the victorious combination of 1918 had been completely dissolved, the new combination of the aggressor states was formed without opposition. By 1936 it existed, and its first important action was to prevent the British, the French, and the Russians from re-creating their own alliance. At Munich in 1938 Hitler compelled Great Britain and France to separate themselves from Russia.[9] The United States had in the meantime persuaded itself, by passing the Neutrality Act, that it must be separated from Britain and France while it became increasingly embroiled with Japan.

[9] The appeasement of Hitler by Mr. Neville Chamberlain and M. Daladier is usually supposed to have consisted in the surrender of the predominantly German-speaking Sudeten territory of Czechoslovakia. But actually the significance of Munich lay in the fact that Britain and France agreed to exclude Russia from a settlement which had the highest strategic consequences in Eastern Europe. The annexation of the Sudetenland by Hitler destroyed the military position of Czechoslovakia, the outer bastion of the Russian defenses. In sacrificing Czechoslovakia to Hitler, Britain and France were really sacrificing their alliance with Russia. This became apparent a year later when they sought in vain to reconstruct the Russian alliance.

The common error in the foreign policy of all the great powers is that they did not take the precaution to become members of an indisputably powerful combination. The aggressor combination was not powerful enough to win: it was powerful enough only to plunge the world into war. The combination of the defenders was not formed until they were on the edge of catastrophe.

Thus we must conclude that in the order of power — in the relationship among the states which are great powers because they can raise great forces and can arm them — the object of each state must be to form a combination which isolates its enemy. From 1935 to 1940 it was Hitler's object to isolate Great Britain. He did not succeed and therefore he must lose the war. Since 1941 it has been the object of the United Nations to separate Germany and Japan and then defeat each of them separately. Every state, whether it is bent on aggression or on pacification, can achieve its purpose only if it avoids being isolated by a combination of the other great states.

To be isolated is for any state the worst of all predicaments. To be the member of a combination which can be depended upon to act together, and, when challenged, to fight together, is to have achieved the highest degree of security which is attainable in a world where there are many sovereign national states.

The world we live in is a world of many sovereign national states, and for the purposes of practical action this condition is given and is unalterable. A Roman Peace, in which one state absorbs and governs all the others, is so completely impossible in our time that we need not stop to argue whether it would be inferno or utopia. If there is to be peace in our time, it will have to be peace among sovereign national states, and the makers of foreign policy can be concerned with no other kind of peace.

Since the first concern of the makers of foreign policy in a sovereign national state must be to achieve the greatest possible security, their object must be to avoid isolation by becoming members of an adequate combination. If they are entirely successful, the adequate alliance to which they belong will either be unchallenged, and they will have peace without fighting for it, or it will be invincible and they will have peace after a victorious war. To be one against the many is the danger, to be among the many against the one is security.

It follows that when the alliance is inadequate because there is an opposing alliance of approximately equal strength, the stage is set for a world war. For then the balance of power is so nearly even that no state is secure. It cannot know whether it would win or would lose the war which it knows is probable. Therefore, it is confronted with the need to calculate the risks of striking first and seizing the advantage of the initiative, or of waiting to be attacked in the hope, usually vain, that it will become too strong to be attacked.

Europe from 1900 to 1914 was in this condition of unstable balance. There was no certain preponderance of force with the Triple Entente or with the Central Powers. The question was put to the test of battle, and it was not until the weight of America was drawn in from the outside that a decision was reached and the war could come to an end. From the rise of Hitler to Munich Europe was again in this condition. No one knew, not Hitler, not Stalin, not Chamberlain or Daladier, the relative strength of the Axis and of the opposing combination. Only when Hitler succeeded at Munich in separating the Franco-British allies from Russia, had he so altered the balance of power in his favor that a war for the conquest of Europe was from his point of view a good risk.

If, then, the object is not only to provide for security against being defeated in war but also to organize a peace which prevents war, the alliance to be adequate must be so dependable and so overwhelmingly powerful that there is no way of challenging it. The combination must be so strong that war against it is not a calculated risk, in which much might be won at a great price, but is instead an obvious impossibility because there would be no chance whatever of winning it.

To form such an overwhelming combination and

maintain it is not easy. That is why peace has never yet
been made universal, and why, when it has been
achieved, it has not lasted. The combinations have
tended to dissolve under the pressure of special interests within their member states. Old powers decline
and new powers emerge. And never yet have statesmen been equal to the task of passing from one order
of power to another without gigantic and prolonged
wars. The cycle of these wars continues until by the
survival of the strongest in the struggle for existence
the new order of power is formed by a preponderant
combination.

6. *The Vulnerability of America*

This nation cannot, as Lincoln said, escape history.[10]
It can, however, at fearful cost misread its own history. It can imagine, until it is smitten by the hard
realities of life, that by some special dispensation of
Providence or some peculiarity of geography it can be
a great power without being involved in the order of
the great powers.

Yet though this illusion is passing, there remains
the practical question of how in fact to form an
American foreign policy which fits the realities of the
American position. In answering it we cannot afford
to deceive ourselves and, therefore, we must begin by

[10] December 1, 1862. Quoted by President Roosevelt
February 12, 1943.

recognizing the uncomfortable fact that our commitments in the outer world are tremendously extended and that our position for fulfilling them is extremely vulnerable.

We are committed to defend at the risk of war the lands and the waters around them extending from Alaska to the Philippines and Australia, from Greenland to Brazil to Patagonia. The area of these commitments is very nearly half the surface of the globe, and within this area we insist that no other great power may enlarge its existing dominion, that no new great power may establish itself.

The area of American defensive commitment is not quite 40 per cent of the land surface of the earth. But it contains a little less than 25 per cent of the population of the earth. The Old World contains 75 per cent of mankind living on 60 per cent of the land of this globe. Thus it is evident that the potential military strength of the Old World is enormously greater than that of the New World. When we look more closely at the facts of power the disparity is even greater. The only arsenal of the New World is in North America; and Canada, which provides an important part of it, is an independent state which has strong ties of interest and of tradition outside the area of our commitments. The Old World, on the other hand, comprises the military states of Britain, Russia, Germany, France, Japan, Italy, and China — all of them arsenals or potential arsenals and each of them with a population used to war and the carrying of arms.

The United States began to mobilize for total war in June 1940. Not until four years later, in 1944, will total mobilization be achieved. Yet in 1943, as the United States works towards a total mobilization, Americans are wondering whether they can maintain eleven million men in the armed forces, construct and sustain a "two ocean" navy, create an air force decisively greater than that of our present enemies, and still take care of the civilian population. There is no doubt that our standards of living are still far higher than they need to be and that we could, if put to it, do all these things and more besides. Nevertheless, the limits of our resources in men and materials are in sight. Yet the combat force we are able to develop is small in comparison with the combat power of the Old World. The total combat power that can be mobilized by Britain, Russia, Germany, Japan, China, France, Italy, Poland, the Central European and the Balkan countries is overwhelmingly superior to that which with the extremest exertion we could possibly mobilize.

These calculations may at first glance seem to some irrelevant because it must seem so unlikely that we should ever have to face the combined power of the Old World. Those who think this are already granting what I am attempting to demonstrate, namely that the New World cannot afford to be isolated against the combined forces of the Old World, and that it must, therefore, find in the Old World dependable friends. They should also remember that as a matter of historic fact this country's vital interests have been threatened by the combined power of the Old World. This threat existed at the conclusion of the great wars a century ago. The threat was averted by the statesmanship of Monroe, Madison, and Jefferson, who seized upon Canning's offer to withdraw Great Britain "from their scale" — that is the European combination — and to shift it "into that of our two continents." [11] Thus experience teaches us that the combination of the Old World against our commitments in the New World is not inconceivable, and wisdom requires that we should never ignore it.

The fact of our military inferiority as an isolated state becomes more portentous when we realize how vulnerable is our strategic position. We have to defend two thirds of the surface of the globe from our continental base in North America. We are an island. South America is an island. The Philippines are islands. Australia is an island. Greenland is an island. All these islands lie in an immense oceanic lake of which the other great powers control the shores. Thus, if we are isolated and have no allies among the great

[11] Jefferson's letter to President Monroe, October 24, 1823.

powers, we have to defend most of the lake without any strategic support upon the mainland from which an attack would be launched. If we knew that the attack was being prepared, we would have no means of striking first to forestall it. We should have to let the combined forces of our enemies prepare themselves at their leisure, and strike when they were ready, and where they chose. This would present us with the dilemma of remaining in an advanced stage of mobilization, or of leaving our vast and scattered domain undefended against surprise attack. But even if we remained highly mobilized our military isolation would bind us to the static defensive. Thus our inferior power in resources and men would be profoundly aggravated by the fact that we would have to disperse our power. But our enemies, having the initiative, could concentrate according to their plans.

If this estimate of our real position seems at first to be incredible, let us remember that it seems incredible only because we have talked about our isolation but have never been so foolish or so unlucky as to be in fact isolated. We were extricated in 1823 from the threat of true isolation by the statesmanship of Canning and Monroe. Their construction lasted until 1917 when we averted the threat of true isolation by Wilson's intervention. In 1940 we were so near to true isolation that for a whole appallingly dangerous year the issue hung precariously upon the valor and skill of the people of Britain, and upon the historic campaign which President Roosevelt waged to arouse this country in time to its awful peril.

The security which Monroe had been able to achieve by diplomacy, Wilson and Roosevelt were unable to accomplish without engaging in war. But in all three instances the United States was faced with the problem of averting the threat of military isolation. The fact that Monroe averted it by diplomacy, and, indeed, by secret diplomacy, and that Wilson and Roosevelt averted it by joining an alliance which was already in the field, has prevented many Americans from perceiving the realities of our position. They do not believe that the consequences of isolation would be so fatal as they would in fact be because, thus far in our history, we have always in the nick of time found adequate allies.

But our luck might not hold. Our improvisations at the eleventh hour might the next time be too little and too late. Thus we must safeguard the future by founding our foreign policy on the undeniable necessity of forming dependable alliances in the Old World.

CHAPTER VII

THE ATLANTIC COMMUNITY

WE COME now to the practical question of what alliances the United States must seek to form: with what other nations and on what terms. If that question can be answered correctly, we shall then be able to see how the level of our postwar armaments, the degree of our military preparedness, and the choice of strategic outposts and bases should be determined. For obviously the American nation cannot remain permanently at the level of armaments which we have set for the year 1943. It is no less obvious that the nation will not, in any future we need consider, disarm. Somewhere between the two extremes the level of our postwar establishments will have to be fixed.

Yet it will be impossible to fix it except in relation to the military power of other states, and on a basis of assured knowledge whether we must regard each of them as partner, potential foe, or uncertain neutral. We must also have this knowledge in order to determine by something more than blind guessing what strategic dispositions we should make. For unless we have organized our own position in the postwar order of the great powers — which means that we have made our alliances — we cannot have a military policy. It is impossible to prepare efficiently against every contingency and all conceivable combinations. It is therefore the business of diplomacy to reduce the uncertainty by forming dependable alliances, in order to limit the number of potential opponents against whom it is necessary to prepare our armaments.

1. Digression on the Balance of Power

I realize, however, that before the case for alliances is conclusively demonstrated, we must pause to examine the notion that it might be possible for the United States to adapt to its own needs the policy of the balance of power by which Britain in the nineteenth century remained aloof from European engagements and yet secure against a combined attack. The theory of this policy was that by supporting the weaker states against the strongest state on the continent Britain could make it impossible for any state to challenge her position outside the continent.

We must note at once, however, that the policy which England applied earlier appeared to work successfully only between the defeat of Napoleon and the rise of Germany as a naval power after 1900.

After the rise of Germany in the twentieth century, it became necessary for Britain to make alliances with France, Russia, and Japan, and to promote, to the best of her ability, the equivalent of an alliance with America. But for these alliances she could not have won the first World War. If she had remained aloof in 1914, she would have had to renounce the policy of the balance of power by assenting to German domination of the continent. Thus, once a really great power had emerged in Europe, Britain could no longer have both security and isolation. In 1914 Britain could have security only by organizing a coalition of allied powers.

After 1919, when it appeared that the German menace had been removed forever, the masters of British policy thought they could revert to the unique security they had enjoyed in the nineteenth century. They not only allowed their alliances to disintegrate but, following the old model, they promoted in its initial phases the revival of the German power. Then, when by 1937–1938 the menace of the German power was upon them, they sought security by abandoning the Russian connection at Munich, in a last vain hope that Germany and Russia would fight and exhaust one another. Thus the attempt to revive the nineteenth-century policy in the altogether different circumstances of the twentieth century was such a disastrous failure that it led directly to the almost catastrophic isolation of Great Britain. In the summer of 1940 France, when it was defeated in Europe, had so lost belief in the British alliance that the undefeated French

Empire deserted Great Britain. Russia, which had been isolated from Europe at Munich, stood aloof, preparing for an isolationist war.

The British form of isolationist policy, which worked temporarily under the unique conditions of the nineteenth century, was proved wholly unsuited to the twentieth century when it was revived. It is not a model which we could afford to follow.

2. *The Victorious Powers*

At the end of this war, if we succeed in destroying the military power of Germany and Japan, there will exist in the world only three great military states — Britain, Russia, and the United States. There will be no others in the immediate postwar world. China, we must in all candor realize, is only potentially a great power of the future. For though the Chinese are brave and numerous and have proved that they can wage war and exert great moral and political influence in Asia, China is not yet an arsenal, and only a state which can raise great forces and equip them is a great power. France will, we may confidently believe, rise again. But there are not enough Frenchmen to make her one of the great powers of the modern world, nor does France possess the resources to become a principal arsenal.

Germany and Japan, we have declared, will not be allowed to become great powers for a long time to come, and if this declaration is to be enforced, then the three surviving great powers — Britain, Russia, and the United States — will have to enforce it. They cannot, however, enforce it unless they are allied for the purpose of enforcing it. If they fail to form the alliance, then it will be because they are potential antagonists. Once that potential antagonism is recognized by their dissolving the alliance which exists in order to wage this war, one or all of the three victors will inevitably move towards arrangements with the defeated powers. As this arrangement develops, the former victors will become competitors for the revival of the power of their former enemies. For unable to enforce the disarmament of the vanquished, because they have now antagonized one another, they will see that the next best form of security will be to make allies of the rearmed vanquished.

Thus the failure to form an alliance of the victors will mean the formation of alliances between the vanquished and some of the victors. This is what happened after 1919: when the victorious alliance dissolved, vanquished Germany made an alliance with victorious Italy and victorious Japan. The state which rejects all alliances will give a high inducement to the other states to form an alliance in which it does not participate. If that state should be America because the American people still want isolation, then we must expect the other powers, who have no such prejudice, to combine for their own security. This will enforce our isolation from Europe, Africa, and Asia. The other powers, then, are certain to consider whether our commitments, which exclude them from the two Americas and from much of the Pacific, are consistent with their interests and their needs. For in these relationships the rule that "if you cannot fight him, you must join him" means that if you do not join him, you will probably have to fight him.

3. *The British-American Connection*

The question then is on the formation of an American alliance with the British Commonwealth and its Empire, and with the Soviet Union.

Let us examine first the project of a British-American alliance.

When we consider the region which the United States must defend, we find that Britain is established within that region as well as outside of it. The defensive region, we must remind ourselves, lies within a line from Greenland to Brazil, and from Alaska to the Philippines.

The Dominion of Canada, with which we have a common land frontier three thousand miles long, is in the geographic center of this region. The only land highway to Alaska passes through Canada. All the short airways to Europe and Asia pass over Canada. To fly to the United Kingdom and to Iceland, to

Scandinavia, to Berlin and Moscow, to Siberia, Japan, and China, the shortest airways are over Canada. Thus the geography of air power links the leading dominion in the British Commonwealth of Nations inseparably with the United States.

But no matter how boldly we allow ourselves to imagine the range and carrying capacity and striking power of the aircraft of the future, two limitations are unalterable.

The first is that aircraft taking off in North America must for civilian purposes be able to land outside of North America — somewhere in Europe, Africa, and Asia. A flight is between two airfields on the ground. For military purposes it is just theoretically conceivable that planes could be built which took off in the United States, attacked in Europe or Asia, and returned to the United States without coming to the ground. But such flights would for the practical future be of no military importance against well-defended objectives across the oceans. So we must conclude that without the use of advanced air bases across the oceans, American air power cannot be developed effectively.

At the utmost, American air power, with assured use of air bases only in North America, would be condemned to the strategy of the passive defense — to waiting for the enemy to strike if, when, and where he chooses. We have already examined the fatal disadvantages of the passive defensive. We need only remind ourselves here that all the positions we have to defend are exposed salients — Greenland and the bulge of Brazil, Alaska and the Philippines. All of them are nearer by air and by sea to some great power of the Old World than they are to the arsenals, training grounds, and recruiting centers of the United States.

The second limitation which we must for the practical future regard as controlling is that American air power cannot be effective without sea power. For it is not practicable by means of the air alone to establish, construct, supply, and defend overseas air bases.

Thus Alaska is no doubt destined to be one of the greatest centers of the air power of the future. But no conceivable development of cargo and transport planes could alone develop and maintain the installations of air power in Alaska. The use of the land highway across Canada and the command of the seas from our Pacific Coast to Alaska are absolutely indispensable.

In regard to Greenland, or a more advanced air base in Iceland, the support of American air power depends upon sea communications. These communications must pass through the North Atlantic ocean passage. On one side of that passage lie the Dominion of Canada and the British colony of Newfoundland, and on the other side of it lie the British Isles. It follows that the security of the northern approaches to the American continent is inseparably related to the sea and air power of Britain. In 1940 when the British Isles were in mortal peril, it was self-evident that the United States could not have held its position in Greenland against German submarines and aircraft established in a conquered Britain. In 1941 it was equally self-evident that Iceland could not be held against a determined attack from German-held Norway without the assured support of British sea and air power. And if Iceland and then Greenland had fallen into enemy hands, the North American continent would have been gravely threatened.

In the South Atlantic, on the approaches to South America, the maintenance of strong sea and air bases on the bulge of Brazil is essential. These bases cannot be maintained by Brazil alone. For Brazil is not an arsenal. The Brazilians have, therefore, to be supported from the United States. But there are no land communications with Brazil. And therefore the strategic defense of the whole South American continent as it faces the Atlantic is dependent upon sea and air communications.

With respect to the arsenal and the primary industrial centers of the world, Brazil is, for commerce and in war, an island. Moreover, it is an island lying nearer to the Old World than to the New. From New York to Belém it is 2975 sea miles. From New York to

Pernambuco it is 3698 sea miles. Now, the distances from South America to all important points under European control are no greater, and to the strategic outposts of European power in Africa they are shorter. Thus the distance from Pernambuco to French Dakar, or from Belém to British Gibraltar or Bathhurst or Freetown, is at least a thousand miles shorter than, is not two thirds so far as, the distance to any comparable strong point of the United States. And if we examine the island outposts of Europe in the South Atlantic — the Spanish Canaries, the Portuguese Cape Verdes, and Britain's Ascension Island — it is evident that the European states are inside the close approaches to South America. We are no nearer than Trinidad, a base useful to the defense of the Panama Canal and the Caribbean, but awkwardly placed and much too distant to be used in the defense of the vast and populous region of South America. Trinidad is a British island, where we have been granted the lease of land for a base because in 1940 we had the sense to realize that the defense of Britain and the defense of America are inseparably a combined undertaking.

Yet even if our sea communications with the bulge of Brazil were assured, we should still be only better prepared to conduct the passive defense. Our bases, including those leased by Britain in 1940, are good only for our passive defense: they cannot be used for the active defense of South America. The jumping-off places for the invasion of South America would still be numerous and so far beyond our reach that we could not snuff out an attack before it was mounted. Here again we find the British power founded on the United Kingdom and projected to Gibraltar and to Bathurst and Freetown in West Africa, and to Capetown in South Africa. The British Isles command the northern entrance to the Atlantic. Gibraltar commands the Mediterranean entrance. Capetown commands the southern entrance from the Indian Ocean. The Falkland Islands command the southern entrance from the Pacific Ocean around Cape Horn. Thus the region we must defend can be attacked only from the region over which Britain commands all the approaches by sea.

Moreover, because the defense of Canada, the greatest of all the British dominions, is inextricably bound up with the defense of the Western Hemisphere, the British vital interest and the American vital interest are complementary and inseparable. Britain must go to the defense of the Americas or the British Commonwealth of Nations would dissolve. America must go to the defense of the United Kingdom and its positions on the other side of the Atlantic, or run the mortal risk of letting a hostile power establish itself in the near approaches to the Western Hemisphere.

The reality of this bond between Britain and America has been tested and demonstrated for more than a century. It compelled Britain in her own interest, it compelled the three Virginian Presidents who had twice been at war with England, to form that concert upon which the Monroe Doctrine has always rested. It compelled both Canada and the United States to enter the two great wars of the twentieth century because in each war the survival of the British power, and therefore the strategic security of the Americas, was at stake.

4. *The British-American Connection in the Pacific*

Once it is clear how indispensable is a British-American alliance in the Atlantic, where our most fundamental interests lie, it will also become clear that the alliance is necessary to the defense of the Pacific. American naval power in the Pacific must, in order to be fully effective, hold securely a chain of bases extending from continental United States through Hawaii, Wake, Guam, and the Japanese mandated islands to the Philippines. It is, however, a line which cannot easily be held securely unless there is an anchor at the other end of this barrier chain of bases. This anchor can be provided only by China. For we must remember that this American line is a very long salient thrust out into Asia. Inevitably, therefore, it is weakest at the end of the salient in the Philippines, and therefore vulnerable if it stands alone.

Our war with Japan has proved how vulnerable it

is. For everything from Wake west has been lost.
Moreover, even if we acknowledge that the unpreparedness of December 7, 1941, will never be permitted to exist again, it is still the fact that the isolated
defense of such a long salient cannot be guaranteed.
When we lost the American line in the winter of
1941–1942, what would we have done if we had had
no allies? What would we have done if China, Britain,
Australia, the Netherlands, and Fighting France had
been neutrals in a Japanese-American war? The whole
campaign of the South Pacific is conducted from British and French bases. The possibility of any direct
attack upon Japan herself depends upon having China
as an ally, and for its full success it depends also upon
having Russia as an ally.

We shall examine our relations with Russia in the
next chapter. Let us note here, however, that we
are powerless alone to open the ports of China. Our
sea power is insufficient. The Chinese armies and
American air forces in China can be built up and
maintained only because India is an ally of China and
of the United States. It is from India that supplies
reach China by air. It is only from India that Burma
can be reconquered and the Burma Road reopened.
But nothing whatever could be done from India if
the British in the United Kingdom were not able to
keep open the sea communications through the Indian
Ocean. Much more can be done from India when the

shorter passage through the Mediterranean, past the British strong positions at Gibraltar, Malta, and Suez, is again open to us.

Is it not undeniable that American commitments in the Atlantic and the Pacific dictate the need for an alliance with the British Commonwealth of Nations and with the Empire?

It has been the geography and the history of North America which have made the British-American connection the crucial point in American foreign relations. To imagine that the connection was invented by schemers and financiers and munitions-makers, and promoted by propagandists, is to deny the facts of geography and the inexorable lessons of historic experience. The real trouble, if we look objectively at our situation and at our history, is not, as some pretend, that American statesmen have been seduced by the British. It is that they have not seen clearly enough and advocated boldly enough the critical and enduring necessity of what Monroe called the concert by agreement — in the plain unadorned language of the obvious truth, of a British-American alliance. As for the propagandists, the trouble with them has been that they have tried to circumvent prejudice and the lack of an understanding of the facts of life by devious, indirect, furtive, emotional circumlocutions. It is better to proclaim frankly that the alliance is necessary, and then to demonstrate the need for it to the common sense of the British, the Canadian, and the American people.

Granting that all alliances have their risks and their inconveniences, is it not a fact that an avowed alliance, an open covenant openly arrived at, is a far healthier relation than a connection which is concealed and denied in time of peace, and then imperatively acted upon under the pressure of catastrophic peril in time of war? No doubt there are, between the British and Americans, conflicting commercial interests at some points, and there are some unhappy memories, and there are social difficulties. But the more openly avowed is the bond of our vital interests, the more clearly we shall see in their true perspective the points of friction and antagonism.

In order to defend the vital interests of both peoples, to make sure that each will survive, responsible men have been compelled since 1914 to gloss over the conflicts of interests which are not vital. Those who emphasize the conflicts — often genuine and important — are in the position of men who irresponsibly risk the greater interest for the sake of the lesser. Only by making sure that the vital common interest in security is invincibly settled can the lesser conflicts of interests be dealt with safely by open discussion and by negotiation. Only when it is certain that the two great systems of states — the British Commonwealth and the American republics — will not go to war with each other, and that neither will permit the other to be destroyed, will there exist the security within which they can safely work out their differences.

5. The Members of the Atlantic Community

The special characteristic of British-American relations is that the British Commonwealth is both inside and outside the area of America's defensive commitments. Canada lies in the midst of it; Australia and New Zealand within it. Thus the overthrow of the American position in the world would mean the break-up of the British Commonwealth. At the same time the citadel of British power is the United Kingdom and the outlying strong points from Gibraltar to Singapore are at the strategic frontiers of the Americas. Thus the overthrow of the British position in the world would mean a revolutionary change in the system of defense within which the American republics have lived for more than a century.

There are twenty American republics and there are, counting Eire and South Africa, six British nations within this community. All of these twenty-six states are self-governing. Though some are much more powerful than others, the sovereignty of their independence is attested by the fact that Eire within the British Commonwealth and the Argentine and Chile within the Pan-American system have been free to remain neutral. They have been free to stay out of the war, even though the war is fought to preserve the system of security which enables them to make this sovereign choice. This is the proof that in fact the British Commonwealth is a commonwealth and not an empire, that the association of American republics is not the façade of United States imperialism.

London was so obviously unable to give orders to the dominions to go to war that no such order was even contemplated, that none, as we see in the case of Eire, was given. Washington gives no orders to its neighbor republics, the proof being that they have freely decided for themselves the time, the degree, and the modes of their neutrality, their non-belligerency, or their adherence to the alliance.

It is the demonstrated fact that London cannot and does not dominate so small, so near, so weak, and so strategically important a dominion as Eire, but must treat with it as a sovereign independent state. It has been demonstrated that the United States cannot and does not dominate on the crucial issue of war and peace American republics like the Argentine and Chile. How insubstantial then is the fear that Britain could dominate a powerful nation like the United States, or be dominated by the United States. Can it then be denied that the British-American connection is, through the facts of geography and the results of historic experience, a community of interest and not a plan of domination or a scheme of empire?

Nor is it, nor can it be, a plan for the combined

domination of the world by the English-speaking nations. We shall see this when we turn to Russia and China. We can see this when we fix our attention upon the other nations which, like Britain, have their vital interests both within and outside the New World. The first of these is France. For a hundred years the only enemy of France has been Germany, and the one frontier France had to defend was her frontier facing Germany. But when France is unable to defend that frontier, as seemed possible in 1917 and was the fact in 1940, it is immediately evident in the New World that the security of France is indispensable to the security of the New World.

The fall of France in 1940 was a conclusive demonstration that France is a member of the great defensive system in which the American republics live. The fall of France laid Spain and Portugal open to the possibility of invasion and domination. This in turn opened up the question of the security of the Spanish and Portuguese island stepping-stones in the Atlantic. The fall of France gave Germany the sea and air bases from which Britain was besieged and American shipping along our Eastern shore and in the Caribbean subjected to a devastating raid. The fall of France uncovered the West Coast of Africa from above Casablanca to Dakar, and opened up the threat, in the event of a German victory in Europe, of a sea-borne and air-borne invasion of South America. The fall of

France had equally momentous consequences in the Pacific. The surrender of French Indo-China to Japan completed the envelopment of the Philippines, and provided the base from which Japan conquered Burma and closed the Burma Road and thus cut off China from her allies.

It follows that France, though a state in continental Europe, is primarily a member of the same community to which the United States belongs. The security of France is an American interest, and the security of the American position is a French interest. The same holds true, and for the same reasons, of Spain and Portugal. The vital interests of the British nations, the American nations, and of the Latin nations on both sides of the Atlantic, and across the Pacific, are so enmeshed by geography, by strategic necessity, and by historic formation that their paramount interests are, when tested in the fires of total war, inseparable. They can fall separately. None of them, not the most powerful, not the two most powerful among them combined — namely the United Kingdom and the United States — can stand comfortably and securely without the others. The proof that clinches the demonstration is that the British nations and the American nations are compelled for their own survival to liberate France and to foster the restoration of the power of France.

Other nations are vitally involved in the system of

security to which we belong. The Netherlands is a small state in Europe with a great empire overseas in the Pacific and with important colonies in the New World. The Netherlands is also one of the outer bastions of both France and Britain. The same is true of Belgium, which has an empire on the Atlantic and is also an outer bastion. Another member of the Atlantic Community is Denmark, which only very recently retired from her colonial possessions in the West Indies, which on the northern approaches to the American continent holds Greenland as a colony and, until recently, was related to Iceland because both had the same king. Norway, too, is a member. For Norway is a country which in relation to Europe is strategically an island lying on the outer limits of the Atlantic world.

Thus the violation of Denmark and Norway, as of the Netherlands and Belgium, was instantly recognized in the Americas and in Britain as a breach in their defenses, and in Norway and in Denmark, as in the Netherlands and Belgium, it was instantly recognized that liberation and restoration depended upon the victory of the British and American nations. Thus when we say that they are members of the same community of interest, we are making an avowal which has been put to the acid test and is no mere amiable generalization.

6. The Inland Sea

If we re-examine the catalogue of nations which are involved in the same system of security, we come upon an interesting and, I believe, a very significant fact. It is that the nations of the New World are still vitally related to precisely those nations of the Old World from which they originated. The settlement of the New World after 1492 was a movement from East to West. The British, the French, the Dutch, the Danes, and we may add the Swedes, moved from the northerly part of the Old World to the northerly part of the New. In the course of their movement they fought many imperialistic wars with one another. But the net result was that the upper part of North America stems from the English and French, and contains important vestiges in New York of the Dutch settlements. The rest of the Americas were settled from the Iberian peninsula, and the two languages of Central and South America are Spanish and Portuguese.

At the end of the eighteenth and the beginning of the nineteenth century most of the nations of the New World won their sovereign independence from the parent nations in the Old World. But the separation, though it is absolute in the realm of self-government, has never existed in the realm of strategic security. The original geographic and historic connections across the Atlantic have persisted. The Atlantic Ocean is not the frontier between Europe and the Americas. It is the inland sea of a community of nations allied with one another by geography, history, and vital necessity.

The members of this community may not all love one another, and they have many conflicting interests. But that is true of any community except perhaps the community of the saints. The test of whether a community exists is not whether we have learned to love our neighbors but whether, when put to the test, we find that we do act as neighbors. By that test all the centuries of experience since the discovery of the Americas have shown that there is peace and order on this side of the Atlantic only when there is peace and order among our neighbors on the other side of the Atlantic. Whenever they have been involved in great wars, the New World has been involved. When they have had peace from great war, as they did have from Waterloo to the first invasion of Belgium, there have been no great international wars that concerned the Americas.

Not what men say, not what they think they feel, but what in fact when they have to act they actually do — that is the test of community. By that test there is a great community on this earth from which no member can be excluded and none can resign. This community has its geographical center in the great basin of the Atlantic.

The security of this community turns upon the relations of the two great powers — Britain and the United States. In this area and at this phase of historic time, they have the arsenals and the military formations necessary to the waging of war. And therefore their alliance is the nucleus of force around which the security of the whole region must necessarily be organized, to which, when their alliance is firm, the other members of the community will in their own interest freely adhere.

CHAPTER VIII

RUSSIA AND THE UNITED STATES

1. A Note on Enlightened Nationalism

WE HAVE taken it for granted that we must discover the true American national interest. We must bear in mind always that there is at stake the life or death of multitudes, victory or defeat in war, the well-being and indeed the survival of the nation. Therefore we must consider first and last the American national interest. If we do not, if we construct our foreign policy on some kind of abstract theory of our rights and duties, we shall build castles in the air. We shall formulate policies which in fact the nation will not support with its blood, its sweat, and its tears. And if, in our search for the true American interest, we fail to find it correctly and to explore its implication exhaustively, our policies will be unworkable in practice because in fact they do not recognize the realities of our position.

In short we shall succeed in so far as we can become fully enlightened American nationalists.

I hope the reader will agree that we have been right in insisting that we can best discern the true national interest not by designing blueprints of the future, but by learning the lessons of experience. This is not, of course, a book of philosophy. But I have written it in the philosophical conviction that the behavior of nations over a long period of time is the most reliable, though not the only, index of their national interest. For though their interests are not eternal, they are remarkably persistent. We can most nearly judge what a nation will probably want by seeing what over a fairly long period of time it has wanted; we can most nearly predict what it will do by knowing what it has usually done. We can best separate appearance from the reality, the transient from the permanent, the significant from the episodic, by looking backward whenever we look forward. There is no great mystery why this should be: the facts of geography are permanent, the movement of history is massive, and the mills of the gods grind slowly; thus the successive generations of men tend to face the same recurrent problems and to react to them in more or less habitual ways. Even when they must adapt themselves to a new situation, their new behavior is likely to be a modification rather than a transformation of their old behavior.

2. *Russian-American Relations in the Past*

The story of Russian-American relations is an impressive demonstration of how unimportant in the determination of policy is ideology, how compelling is national interest. In a classic paper on this subject, Mr. DeWitt Clinton Poole has shown that Americans have never in all their history liked "the governments which the Russians have permitted to rule over them." [1] They have disliked the Czarist autocracy and they have disliked the Soviet dictatorship. The Czars returned the compliment by regarding the American democracy as a bad revolutionary example, and in fact Russia was the last of the great powers to grant diplomatic recognition to the United States. The Czar refused to receive Dana, the American Minister, in 1780. Alexander III accepted the credentials of John Quincy Adams only in 1809, and Russia did not sign its first treaty of commerce with us until 1832.

Today *we* are the conservative state. The Soviets have regarded America as a capitalist, imperialist state, and therefore antagonistic to their social order. Except for the few months between the fall of the Czars in March 1917 and the bolshevik revolution in November 1917, the political ideologies of the two nations have always been poles apart.

Nevertheless, though these profound differences of

[1] I am profoundly indebted to Mr. DeWitt Clinton Poole's paper on "Russia and the United States" which was published in the issue of *New Europe* for September 1941. Almost all the facts and above all the theory of Russian-American relations are derived from Mr. Poole's paper.

ideology have always meant that their diplomatic intercourse was exceedingly difficult, Russia and the United States have usually, each in its own interest, supported one another in the critical moments of their history. Even in the period from the formation of the Holy Alliance in 1815 to Monroe's Message in 1823, the profound ideological antagonism did not prevent the Czar's foreign minister from deciding that in the matter of Russian territorial claims as far south as Bodega Bay in California "it would be best for us to waive all discussions upon abstract principles of right." A compromise was worked out limiting Russian rights to a line at Sitka in Alaska.

The enduring element in Russian-American relations is that in critical times each nation has always been "for the other a potential friend in the rear of potential enemies." [2] In the War of Independence the Continental Congress sought the assistance of Russia, and Russia practised, entirely in her own interest, an armed neutrality which favored the colonies. In 1863, at the darkest moment of the Civil War, there occurred the Polish insurrection against Russia. Both Britain and France were considering giving support to the Confederacy in America and to the Polish rebellion. In spite of American ideological sympathy with the Polish national rebellion, Lincoln and Seward refused to intervene diplomatically against Russia. In

[2] Poole, *op. cit.*

spite of Russian antipathy to the American democracy, the Czar's government stated, in the official journal of the Foreign Office, that the preservation of the United States was an imperative necessity for Russia, and backed up this declaration by dispatching a squadron of warships from its Baltic fleet to New York and from the Pacific squadron to San Francisco. This gesture had its effect in London and in Paris, warning them not to recognize the Confederacy or to support the Polish insurrection. "I did not do what I did for love of the United States," said the Czar Alexander, "but for Russia." [3]

In the first World War antipathy to Czarist Russia was the chief sentimental objection to the ideological claims of the Triple Entente, and, later, American antipathy to the bolshevik revolutionary terror was intense and almost universal. Nevertheless, regardless of bolshevism, the American policy was firmly opposed to the dismemberment of Russia, and what is more, the bolshevik leaders knew it and counted upon it. Thus in May 1918 Lenin addressed the Central Executive Committee at Moscow, saying that "an inevitable conflict will arise between Japan and America

[3] Dow, Roger, "The Tradition of Russo-American Partnership," published by American Defense Harvard Group, Widener Library, Harvard University. Both in the Crimean War and in the Near Eastern crisis of 1878, American neutrality was belligerently benevolent to Russia, no doubt in order to clip the power of Britain.

for the supremacy of the Pacific and its coasts. The conflicting interests of the two imperialistic countries, now screened by an alliance against Germany, check the movement of Japanese imperialism against Russia." [4] Lenin's prediction was correct. American and Japanese forces occupied Vladivostok and the Maritime Province of Siberia in 1918, and the controlling reason for sending the American forces was to watch and to restrain Japan. When the American forces were withdrawn, the United States insisted that the Japanese force be withdrawn also, and at the Washington Disarmament Conference of 1922, Secretary Hughes finally prevailed upon Japan. In spite of Russian bolshevism, in spite of Japan's having been an associate in the war against Germany, we acted upon the belief that the territorial integrity of Russia was a vital interest of the United States.[5]

[4] Quoted by Poole, *op. cit.* U. S. Foreign Relations, 1918, Russia I: 303 and 529.

[5] For the same reasons the United States withheld full *de jure* recognition of Lithuania, Latvia, Esthonia, until July 1922, and then granted it reluctantly and with the belief that it was provisional. Though the United States government sympathized with their national aspirations, the American High Commissioner, Mr. Evan Young, who recommended recognition, stated at the time that "it is entirely possible, or even probable, that some time in the indefinite future these states may once again become an integral part of Russia — however, until that time comes,

Historic experience shows, then, that Russia and the United States, placed "on opposite sides of the globe," have always been antagonistic in their political ideology, always suspicious that close contact would be subversive. Yet each has always opposed the dismemberment of the other. Each has always wished the other to be strong. They have never had a collision which made them enemies. Each has regarded the other as a potential friend in the rear of its potential enemies.

3. *Russian-American Relations in the Future*

May this historic relationship be expected to continue after the destruction of the military power of Germany and Japan? The answer must be, whatever the future may bring, that we are at a decisive turning point in our relations with Russia. It is a turning point comparable with that which we reached about 1900. Then the extension of American commitments to the Philippines and China coincided with the emergence of Germany as the greatest power in continental Europe. Two wars with Germany to preserve

---

they will be able to maintain their political stability, and with that their independence. . . . Admitting that from our point of view, a strong Russia is greatly to be desired, it is still difficult for an observer here to suggest any course of action other than the immediate recognition of these States." (U. S. Foreign Relations, 1922, II: 871.)

the security of the Atlantic, and a war with Japan to fulfill our commitments in Asia, have been the result of the profound changes that occurred at the beginning of the century.

It is the assumption now that this war will mean the conclusive defeat of both Germany and Japan. What do we mean by a conclusive defeat? We mean that as a result of the defeat Germany will never again be able to make a bid for the mastery of Europe and of the transatlantic region of American security; that Japan will never again be able to seek to make an empire over China and the Indies. Naturally we ask ourselves whether there is any reasonable ground for believing that their defeat can be as conclusive as that. Or is it more reasonable to assume that our present enemies will rise to fight again, as Germany did twenty years after Versailles?

We can say that nations have in the past been conclusively defeated. Spain was so conclusively defeated in the sixteenth century that it never again was a great power. France was so conclusively defeated by Russia and Britain in 1812–1814 that it was never again able to seek a Napoleonic Empire. The Spanish nation did not cease to exist. The French nation continued to play a great part in the world, and the ghost of Bonaparte walked again in Napoleon III. Nevertheless, the retreat from Moscow and the defeat at Waterloo were conclusive. What made them conclusive? It was that in the nineteenth century the French potential for war declined first in comparison with Britain's, and then in comparison with the war potential of a unified and industrialized Germany with its rapidly growing population.

In this sense it is a reasonable expectation that Germany and Japan are in the last phase of their last attempt at world empire. For just as the war potential of France declined relatively to that of Britain and Germany, so now Germany's is in decline relatively to that of industrialized Russia and of America plus Britain. The same expectation holds for Japan in that the postwar world is likely to see China industrialized, Russia in Siberia become immensely stronger, and the United States conscious of its military potential. This does not mean that Germany and Japan will disappear from the scales of world power. But it does mean that they may never again be great powers of the first magnitude.

If this assumption is correct, then Russian-American relations will no longer be controlled by the historic fact that each is for the other a potential friend in the rear of its potential enemies. Russia will, on the contrary, be the greatest power in the rear of our indispensable friends — the British, Scandinavian, Dutch, Belgian, and Latin members of the Atlantic Community. In Asia, Russia will be our nearest neighbor across the Northern Pacific and by air over the Polar regions; Russia will be the nearest neighbor of China.

Thus the question in Europe is whether Russia will seek to extend her power westward into Europe in such a way that it threatens the security of the Atlantic states. The question in the Pacific is whether as nearest neighbors by land, sea, and air, the United States and Russia will move towards rivalry or towards a common ground of understanding. The two questions are inseparable because, as the Russian statesmen have so often insisted, peace is indivisible. We should, therefore, be lacking in candor and realism if we did not face the fact that the crucial question of the epoch that we are now entering is the relationship between Russia and that Atlantic Community in which Britain and the United States are the leading military powers.

4. *The American Interest in the European Settlement*

Out of this question there arises America's vital interest in the settlement of European affairs, and it is plain, I submit, that our grand objective must be a settlement which does not call for a permanent American military intervention in Europe to maintain it. I am not speaking of the force needed to make the defeat of Germany conclusive, but, to be absolutely explicit, the force to maintain the European order against Russia after Germany has ceased to be the great power of continental Europe. A settlement which was such that it could be maintained only by aligning

American, and therefore also British, military power against Russia in Europe would set the stage inexorably for a third World War in Europe and in Asia as well.

Russia and the Atlantic Community have, therefore, a profound common interest in a European settlement which will maintain itself without bringing them into conflict. We must admit that nations are not always enlightened enough to know what their real interests are, and to do what their real interests dictate. In the twentieth century none of us has had such an enlightened policy, and twice we have become involved, without being prepared for them, in great wars, and once we have not known how to make peace though we were victorious. We might fail again because it takes many enlightened nations to make peace, whereas one nation can start a war. But this at least we can say: if we fail to make peace after this war, we shall know that we have not made it. So we shall be immediately forewarned that we must prepare for the next war. In 1919 we did not know that, and that is why we not only failed to make peace, but failed so lamentably to be prepared for war.

We shall be forewarned this time because the objective test of whether there is to be peace or war will be whether the borderland between Russia and the Atlantic states is settled by consent or by pressure, dictation, and diplomatic violence. This borderland begins with Finland in the North and includes Sweden, and extends through Poland, the Danubian nations, the Balkan nations, to Turkey, and it includes Germany. If in this region the effort to settle territorial boundaries and to decide what governments shall be recognized discloses deep and insoluble conflicts between Russia's conception of her vital interests and that of the Western Allies, then every nation will know that it must get ready and must choose sides in the eventual but unavoidable next war.

It is not possible for the United States, and therefore it will not be possible for Great Britain either, to impose and maintain a settlement in this region by military force. Our power is on the sea and in the air, not on the land, and our interest in the interior of the European continent is indirect, concerned with it vitally only as it bears upon our relations with great world powers like Germany in the receding past, like Russia in the emergent future.

It follows that we cannot agree again to the underlying conception of the Versailles settlement which treated the border region as a military barrier, as the *cordon sanitaire*, between Russia and the rest of Europe. The barrier has no military value. Germany broke through it easily. Russia could break through it easily. The barrier cannot be reconstructed. For Britain, liberated France, and America will not and cannot stand guard on the barrier. They are not strong

enough. They cannot permit Germany to stand guard
on it because to reconstitute the German military
power is to alienate Russia fatally and thus to leave
France and Britain exposed, without Russian help, to
the power of reconstituted Germany. Finally and
conclusively the barrier cannot be reconstructed because Russia, emerging from this war the great military
power of Europe whereas in 1918 she was prostrate,
can erase the barrier by forming an alliance with
post-Nazi Germany.

To encourage the nations of Central and Eastern
Europe to organize themselves as a barrier against
Russia would be to make a commitment that the
United States could not carry out. A barrier implies
that in conducting their relations with Russia the
barrier states may count upon the armed support of
the Atlantic powers. Yet the region lies beyond the
reach of American power, and therefore the implied
commitment would be unbalanced and insolvent. We
should be in the position of promising these nations
a protection we are unable to provide, of encouraging
them to pursue policies which we are unable to under-
write, and to take risks which might have consequences
which we cannot insure them against.

Does this mean that Poland, the Danubian states, and
the Balkan states have no prospect of assured independence and that they are destined inexorably to become satellites of Russia or to be incorporated into

the Soviet Union? The question cannot be answered categorically at this time. We may say, I believe, that these states would have no prospect of independence if America and Britain, working with the governments-in-exile, were to attempt to reconstitute them as the outposts of a Western Coalition against Russia. When the war ends, the Russians will almost certainly have an overwhelming preponderance of military force in this region, and it is inconceivable that the Red Army, if it liberates these peoples from the Nazi conquerors, will permit governments operating from London and Washington to organize anti-Russian states on the Russian border. The very attempt to do this, even the suspicion of an attempt, is bound to revive the bitter memories of the Allied intervention of 1919 in the Russian Civil War. Then the question will not be how firmly we can guarantee the independence of these states, but whether Russia will permit them to exist at all as independent states.

Moreover, these states are by no means homogeneous or united. They have many deep differences among themselves. Therefore, the attempt of some of them to play a part in anti-Russian power politics will almost certainly cause others among them to make power alliances with Russia. If Poland and Hungary, for example, sought to make themselves outposts of an anti-Russian barrier, the probabilities are that the Czechs, the Bulgars, and perhaps the Rumanians would

quickly come to terms with Russia. What then would
be the prospect for Britain and America? Would they
furnish to Poland and Hungary arms to equip armies?
If they did, they would be directly embroiled with
Russia all over the world. If they did not, how could
Poland and Hungary find the equipment?

It follows that the existence of these borderland
states depends upon their neutralization in the realm
of power politics. This is not an easy solution, for
their whole historic tradition runs counter to it. They
are the fragments of three ancient empires — the Russian, the Hapsburg, and the Turkish — and the political assumptions and the politics of their governing
classes have been formed in the power politics of the
empires of which until recently they were the parts.
Thus, unlike Switzerland and the Scandinavian states,
they do not have the ideas and the usages which are
necessary to the practice of genuine neutrality.

Nor have they had the opportunity to acquire them.
They achieved their independence recently as a result of the conflict of empires. The expulsion of Turkey from Europe, the defeat of the Russian Empire in
1916 and of the Austro-Hungarian Empire in 1918,
brought them independence. Thus their politically-
minded men habitually assume that salvation for small
states is to be found only in seizing the opportunities
opened up by the conflict of great powers.

The question is whether after the defeat and disarmament of Germany and Italy the fact that there is no conflict of great powers in this region, nor even a balance of power, can be made to mean that these states will change their basic political assumptions, retire from power politics, and seek a neutralized role like that of the Scandinavians and the Swiss.

Law, it has been said, and not power, is the defense of small states. It would seem that the hope of a good settlement on Russia's western borderlands depends upon whether the border states will adopt a policy of neutralization, and whether Russia will respect and support it. The best interests of the United States would be served by such a solution. It would not bring us or the members of the Atlantic Community into conflict with Russia. It would give Poland, the Danubian states, and the Balkans the only form of security we are able to offer them, and it would give Russia security resting on the fact that the nations of Central and Eastern Europe, after Germany has been disarmed, could not become the spearheads of a Western Coalition.

5. *Russia and the United States in the Pacific*

Our relations with Russia in Europe are indirect, twice removed in fact, since between us and Russia lie first the border nations and then the members of the Atlantic Community. But with Russia in Asia our relations will become, after the destruction of

Japanese power, direct and of the highest consequence. In fact, here Russia is physically the nearest to us of any great power, excepting only Canada as a member of the British Commonwealth. The farthest of the Aleutians is only a few hundred miles by sea from Petropavlovsk in Kamchatka. Alaska is nearer to Siberia than it is to the United States. The shortest airways from America to China pass over Russian territory. It is no farther from Nome to Yakutsk by air than from Nome to Seattle, or from Fairbanks to the Maritime Provinces than to Detroit. With Japan eliminated, the western part of the North Pacific is under Russian control, and the eastern part under American. If, as most airmen believe, the Arctic Ocean is to be one of the principal airways of the future, then the United States, Canada, the United Kingdom, and Russia are the four nations which will control those airways.

Our relations with Russia can no longer be regulated, then, by the old rule that each is to the other a potential friend in the rear of its potential enemies. The defeat of Japan and the advent of the age of polar flying will make Russia and the United States neighbors. Is there a conflict of vital interest which could cause enmity? One thing can be said at once: there is no boundary dispute, no American territory which Russia covets, no Russian territory to which the United States has ever laid any claim whatever. Alaska was obtained from Russia by purchase, certainly without any compulsion on our part, and there has never been any indication that the Russians regretted the sale. Thus if there is a potential conflict of interest, the conflict cannot arise directly.

That brings us to China. For manifestly the peace of the Pacific has turned and will turn upon China. All the international wars of the Pacific, including the war we are now waging, have turned upon China, and the future of China will for good or evil determine the future in the whole great basin of the Pacific.

CHAPTER IX

CHINA AND THE UNITED STATES

1. The China Connection

THE ONE certain thing which can be said of the future in the Pacific is that there is no prospect of a settled and stabilized international order. In the West it may be difficult to achieve general security. But at least there is visible the general shape of things that could be made to come to pass. There is the Atlantic Community organized for its security. There is Germany conclusively estopped from attempting to break up the Atlantic Community or to conquer Russia, and thus constrained to become eventually a non-aggressive state. There is the neutralized borderland. There is Russia strong and safe for its internal development within its natural and accepted western limits. A settled order of this general character is a practical possibility if the statesmen and their peoples can rise to the occasion and take advantage of the fact that the vital interest of all the states concerned is to find security in a stabilized order.

But in the East the whole situation is dynamic, and

set for epoch-making change of which we cannot foresee the limits. For the objective of the Pacific war, and its most probable consequence, is the emergence of China as a new great power in the modern world. The emergence of any new great power upon the stage of history must of necessity affect the whole course of history. For how can we calculate the course of a great power which has never existed but is about to appear? All that we know is that with independence, unity, and the industrialization of their country, the vast numbers of the Chinese nation should in the course of time organize themselves as a great power.

The United States has since 1899 been committed to the task of fostering this development. As soon as the United States became a power in the Far East by occupying the Philippines, the American government committed itself to opposing the dismemberment of China into spheres of imperialist influence.[1] This was the Open Door Policy. With some temporary deviations and some lapses, the United States adhered to this policy, and finally became engaged in the present war because it would not renounce the policy.

For the issue which precipitated the Japanese-American War in 1941 was the refusal of the United

[1] For an illuminating study of the roots of this policy in the nineteenth century cf. Nathaniel Peffer, *Basis for Peace in the Far East*, Ch. 3.

States to give Japan a free hand in the conquest of China. The Japanese proposal of November 20, 1941, for a general settlement in the Pacific was rejected by the United States government on November 26 because Japan demanded the discontinuance of American aid to China as the price of halting her armed advance in Southeastern Asia and of withdrawing eventually from Southern French Indo-China.[2] The irreconcilable issue was in China, and not in Indo-China or in the Netherlands Indies or in Malaya.[3] The price of peace with Japan was the assent of the United States to the Japanese conquest of China.

On its face, as Peffer points out, it is almost inexplicable that "a people coming from Europe to the eastern shore of a fresh and uninhabited continent three thousand miles broad should find themselves in a few generations committed in the lives of their sons and their fortunes to the affairs of a country almost six thousand miles from the western shore of that continent, after consciously having resolved throughout their history to cut themselves off from the affairs of the continent from which they sprang. . . . Yet with Asia, with which there was and could be no community of any kind, not the most tenuous link, there has been conscious, direct, willed concern. With Europe, no en-

[2] Cf. *Peace and War, U. S. Foreign Policy 1931–1941,* published by the Department of State, pp. 133–138.
[3] Cf. Peffer, *op. cit.,* p. 14.

tanglement; with Asia, active participation in all its remote, exotic politics." [4]

Mr. Peffer asks "Why the contrast?" His answer is that the compelling motive of American concern with Asia was, as stated by President Fillmore in 1849, "the consideration . . . of the great trade which must at no distant day be carried on between the western coast of North America and Eastern Asia." But this in itself does not explain why the United States could for so long have been so conscious of its trading interests in Asia and so unconscious of its security in relation to Europe. To explain that we have again to remind ourselves of Monroe's concert with Britain which for at least seventy-five years made it unnecessary for Americans to think about Europe. [5] The American expansion across the Pacific to Asia was possible because of American security in the Atlantic.

Thus in the course of events the United States became committed to the conviction that China should cease to be a colony dominated by foreign empires and it should become an integrated and independent power, and in fact a great military power. Victory in this war will fulfill that commitment at least to the point of giving China a free chance to make herself a great power, and probably also to the point of our

[4] *Op. cit.*, p. 30.
[5] Cf. Chapter III, section 2.

rendering China active assistance in making herself a great power.

2. The Instability of Eastern Asia

In Eastern Asia there will then be Russia, our nearest neighbor, and China, for whom we have waged a great war to insure her the chance to become the great power which her numbers, her resources, and her ancient culture make it possible for her to become. We cannot see further than that now. For China, Russia in Siberia, and North America as it reaches towards Asia are all of them at the beginning of a new and historic phase of industrialization, and of the development of the newer forms of military power by sea and in the air.

Moreover, the emergence of China as a great power will change the whole order of power within which lie the Philippines, the Indies, Australasia, Malaya, and the immense and awakening sub-continent of India. We cannot know now what a great Chinese power in this region of the world portends, and we cannot afford to freeze our ideas about a situation which will only gradually unfold itself. All we can do is to act on the assumption that the conditions which for half a century have made the integrity and security of China a vital interest of the United States will, as China becomes a great power, make the security of the United States a vital interest of China.

What we must realize, however, is that the defeat of Japan will be the beginning and not the end of profound historic change in the Eastern world. The one end which it is impossible to achieve is a stabilization now in the Chinese lands, in India, and in the Moslem countries, like that which we can hope to achieve in the Western World.

If stabilization of at least half the world is impossible in our time, then it follows that only by participating in the organization of sufficient lawful power can we hope to hold the impending and unpredictable changes within peaceable channels.

CHAPTER X

THE GENERAL ORDER OF
THE NATIONS

1. The Nuclear Alliance

THE PRESENT association of the United States with
Britain, Russia, and China is not a new departure. We
have seen how for more than a century, whenever our
vital interests were at stake, American foreign relations have always been primarily our relations with
Britain, with Russia, and with China. Our relations
with all other states have followed upon and have been
governed by our relations with those three. In the conduct of American foreign policy our position has been
solvent, our power adequate to our commitments, in
so far as we were in essential agreement with these
three states.

None of them, we may observe, is a European state.
We must ponder this fact. For it may throw light
upon the famous statement in Washington's Farewell
Address that: —

Europe has a set of primary interests which to
us have none or a very remote relation. Hence

she must be engaged in frequent controversies, the causes of which are essentially foreign to our concerns.

When these words were spoken on September 17, 1796, Napoleon was conducting his first campaign of aggression, the invasion of Italy. His conquest of the continent was still in the future, as was his threat to invade England and his actual invasion of Russia. The war which Washington knew about had all the appearance of being a purely *European* war, which to us had none or a very remote relation. Sixteen years later, however, Napoleon was the master of Europe, and had struck outside of Europe into Russia. The United States had become involved in a local war with England. Yet while America was at war, we find Jefferson, the author of the phrase "no entangling alliances," writing on January 1, 1814, that "surely none of us wish to see Bonaparte conquer Russia, and lay thus at his feet the whole continent of Europe. This done, England would be but a breakfast. . . . Put all Europe into his hands, and he might spare such a force, to be sent in British ships, as I would as leave not have to encounter." Jefferson was writing a private letter in wartime [1] and he added: "I have gone into this explanation, my friend, because I know you will not carry my letter to the newspapers, and because I am

---

[1] To Thomas Leiper, 14 Jefferson 41, 43.

willing to trust to your discretion the explaining me to our honest fellow laborers and the bringing them to pause and reflect . . . on the extent of the success we ought to wish to Bonaparte, and with a view to our own interests only."

We see here how the very men who laid down the rule of nonparticipation in European politics really thought about our foreign relations. They were aware that when there was a power in Europe which threatened to *come out of Europe* and conquer Britain, which is at one of the limits of Europe, or to conquer Russia which is at the other limit, our interests were vitally involved. If we read our history, not as the conventional historians have written it, and not as our lesser statesmen have talked about it, but as in fact Americans have enacted it, we find, I submit, that while our concern has not been with *European* affairs, we have always been concerned with *world* affairs. Our primary relations have been, and are, with the extra-European powers, and with Europe itself only as some power inside of Europe threatens to disrupt the order of things outside of Europe. Thus, if we think as clearly and exactly about American interests as Jefferson, even in the midst of a jingoistic war, was able to think, we shall see that the traditional American policy against being involved in European affairs is not in the last analysis inconsistent with the consolidation of America's vital interest in the world.

Our primary interest in Europe, as shown during the Napoleonic and the two German Wars, is that no European power should emerge which is capable of aggression outside of the European continent. Therefore our two natural and permanent allies have been and are Britain and Russia. For they have the same fundamental interest — to each of them a matter of national life or death — in preventing the rise of such a conquering power in Europe. And that is why Britain and Russia, though they have been at odds on the Near East, the Middle East, and in Asia, have been allies against Napoleon, against William II, and against Hitler.

Here then, founded on vital interest which has been tested and proved in the course of generations, is the nuclear alliance upon which depends the maintenance of the world order in which America lives. Combined action by America, Britain, and Russia is the irreducible minimum guarantee of the security of each of them, and the only condition under which it is possible even to begin to establish any wider order of security.

The formation of this nuclear alliance must in our thinking and in our action take precedence over all other considerations. For without it we cannot make good our existing commitments in the Atlantic and in the Pacific. Without it, our commitment in the Philippines remains a salient, exceedingly difficult to defend against a resurgent Japan or against a combination of powers in Eastern Asia. Without this nuclear alliance, our commitment in South America is open to challenge, if not by direct conquest from Europe and Africa, then by infiltration and conspiracy. Without it, the two oceans and the airways to the north and the south are perilously open and uncertain, since the ports and landing fields beyond would be in uncertain hands.

Only by the formation of this nuclear alliance — whatever we choose to call it, no matter how we choose to seal it — can American foreign policy be said to have balanced our commitments with a safe margin in reserve. We need make no apologies then because we put this first thing first. American foreign relations must be made solvent before the United States can afford to issue any more promissory notes.

Furthermore, we should not have learned the lessons of our failures in the past, especially the lesson of the failure of the League of Nations, if in our projects for organizing world peace we did not fix our attention first of all upon the powers capable of organizing it. Blueprints, covenants, contracts, charters, and declarations do not create living associations. They merely formulate, regulate, ratify, develop, and guide the action of men or groups of men who already have the will to associate themselves. It is not, for example, the marriage laws which make the family, but the

union of a man and a woman who in accordance with
these laws then found a family. It was not the Constitution which made the American union, but the con-
stituent states which adopted it in order to form a
more perfect union.

The will of the most powerful states to remain allied is the only possible creator of a general international order.

2. *The Justification of Insisting upon It*

There will be many, I realize full well, who will
feel that this insistence upon the security of the vital
interests of the most powerful states involves an il-
liberal and even a brutal neglect of the rights of the
weaker nations and of their intrinsic importance to
civilization itself. I ask their indulgence until the argument is concluded. We shall see why the nuclear alliance must be liberal in its policy if it is to endure.

But if we are to prove this convincingly, and not
merely to state it rhetorically, there must be no doubt
in our minds why as Americans we must insist upon
beginning with the security of the vital interests of
the United States. It is that for half a century the
United States has so neglected its vital interests that
it was incapable of defending them adequately, or of
carrying through any measures whatsoever to maintain the peace of the world. For fifty years no nation
has been more liberal in its words than has been the

United States; none neglected its own interests so dangerously, or contributed less to realizing the ideals it so assiduously preached.

So I make no apology for seeking to define the American foreign policy on which the American people could again become united because it conforms rigorously to American interests. I see no way of our being able to contribute anything to anybody else until we have become fully conscious again of our own interests and feel prepared to maintain them. . . . And I do not doubt that our allies and our friendly neighbors will, as they consider the matter, greatly prefer an American foreign policy founded on an enlightened conception of our own national interest to the ambiguous platitudes with which we have regaled them for the past fifty years.

Nor need we shrink from insisting that the precondition of a better world order is a nuclear alliance of the three powerful military states which will emerge victorious from the present war. They are the states upon which depends the deliverance of Europe from the Nazi despotism, and of the Far East from the empire of Japan. It has needed the combined force of all three of these states, and the utmost exertion of their power, to make the deliverance possible. No one of them, no two of them, could have done it. Why, then, should we hesitate to say that anything less than this combination of great powers is insufficient to preserve order against aggression in the world? Will anyone presume to argue that to dissolve this combination again would promote the liberty of the peoples who have been conquered, or would make secure the order which has been shattered by two devastating world wars?

It is only around this strong nuclear alliance that a wider association of many nations can constitute itself. If that condition is accepted, and once it is accepted, it will become evident that the combination of the great powers cannot, despite their common vital interests, be made to hold together except as they respect the liberties of the other peoples and promote them by the maintenance of law.

I believe it can be demonstrated as conclusively as anything can be demonstrated in human affairs that Britain, Russia, America, and China as she becomes a great state, cannot remain allies and partners unless they use their power, separately and in combination, to maintain liberty through law.

3. *The Binding Condition of Unity*

We must begin by remembering that Britain, Russia, and America are allies, not by conscious choice but under the compulsion of their common enemies. They have been compelled, as I have tried to show, to become allies whenever a really formidable aggressive power emerged which threatened to break out of Europe into the outer world. Nevertheless, when there is no such enemy which threatens their national existence, the need for their alliance becomes submerged. Their lesser, their separate and conflicting, interests are then free to assert themselves. The greater the peril from the outside, the closer is their union: the greater their security, the more their differences come to the surface.

The unconditional surrender of Germany and of Japan is bound, therefore, to leave all the Allies with an immediate sense of mortal peril averted; and this will reduce the compulsion that binds the alliance together. There will then be opened up disputable secondary questions which push apart the members of the alliance. This has always happened in wars won by a coalition. It happened at the Congress of Vienna, and because of it Talleyrand's diplomacy was so successful. It happened at the Peace Conference in 1919, when the victorious alliance had in fact become dissolved even before peace had been made with the enemy. It can and it may happen again, as we have seen in the winter of 1943, when the first prospects of victory have already opened up fissures among the Allies.

These fissures will tend to become wider and deeper the more any one of the great powers seeks to aggrandize itself either at the expense of one of the other great powers, or at the expense of their smaller allies.

Thus an American policy of imperialist aggrandizement at the expense of the British Empire would impair profoundly, if it did not destroy, the Atlantic Community. It would become necessary for Britain to look for her security in some combination which thwarted American aggrandizement.

By the same token, a British policy which rested on the refusal to recognize the necessary changes in the colonial and imperial system of the nineteenth century would raise up against Britain insurgent forces in Asia, the Middle East, and Africa. Britain could not count upon American support in resisting these forces, and almost certainly she would have to count upon Russian and Chinese encouragement of these forces.

By the same token again, a Russian policy of aggrandizement in Europe, one which threatened the national liberties of her neighbors, would inexorably be regarded as such a threat to Britain and America that they would begin to encourage the nations which resisted Russia. In Asia, a Russian policy of aggrandizement against China would disrupt Russian-American relations in the North Pacific and, in the coming air age, across the top of the globe. On the other hand, an anti-Russian policy in which Britain, America, and the European states sought, as they did in 1919, to blockade and even to disrupt Russia would provoke Russian communist intervention to counteract it.

And by the same token, also, a Chinese policy of aggrandizement in India, Malaya, Indo-China, and the Netherlands Indies would encounter opposition from Britain, from America, from Australia and New Zealand, from France and the Netherlands.

The fissures opened by any one or all of these tendencies to aggrandizement would soon become a breach. This would be followed inevitably and immediately by competition among the Allies to win over to their side the vanquished nations. This would be done by restoring their power. In Europe the separated Allies would bid against one another for the favor of Germany. In Asia, they would bid for the favor of Japan. Thus because aggrandizement had made them rivals, they would restore the aggressor powers which had threatened them. The postwar era would thus be transformed, as the late Frank Simonds observed of the early thirties, into a pre-war era.

For these reasons it is evident that a nuclear alliance of Britain, Russia, America, and, if possible, China, cannot hold together if it does not operate within the limitations of an international order that preserves the national liberties of other peoples. The three, or the four, great powers will not remain united against the revival of German and Japanese military power if they become rivals in the domination of Central and Eastern Europe or of the dependent and colonial regions of Asia and Africa.

Nor could the nuclear allies, as some may fear, combine to oppress and exploit the rest of mankind. For, in the last analysis, the resistance of the rest of mankind would disrupt the alliance: one or the other of the great powers would find that its interests and its *Russia* sympathies lay with the peoples resisting oppression.

Nor could the nuclear allies divide the globe into spheres of influence which each was free to dominate and exploit separately. For no spheres of influence can be defined which do not overlap, which would not therefore bring the great powers into conflict. Where in Europe, for example, could a sphere of influence be fixed which separated Britain and Russia into convenient imperialist compartments? On which side of the line would the Scandinavian countries lie? If on the Russian, then the sea and air approaches to Britain are insecure; if on the British, then the sea and air approaches to Russia are insecure. Where in Africa could a line of demarcation be drawn when, in fact, the defense of South America is dependent upon the presence of friendly powers in North and West Africa, when in fact the security of the Mediterranean is also dependent upon the control of North and West Africa? Where can a sphere of influence be defined in the East which makes secure China, the British nations in Australasia, and the American commitment in the Philippines?

Thus it is as impossible for the Allied great powers

to divide up the world and then rule it as it is for them to combine in order to dominate the world. The inexorable logic of their alliance demands that they recognize the liberties of the peoples outside the alliance. For in no other way can they avoid becoming rivals and then enemies for the domination of these other peoples. In no other way but by supporting a world-wide system of liberty under law can they win the consent, earn the confidence, and insure the support of the rest of the world in the continuation of their alliance.

The order which they originate because it is necessary to their own vital security can, therefore, be perpetuated only if they act so as to gain and to hold the good will of the other peoples. Delivering the weaker states from the Nazi and Japanese conquest will not in itself hold their good will. For the memory of the deliverance will become obscured by what happens afterwards. Their own concept of their own interest, rather than gratitude, is for all masses of peoples the motive which determines their actions. The gratitude of the liberated to the victorious powers will, therefore, continue only if the great powers remain united enough to keep the peace of the world against aggressors and at the same time become liberal enough so that there is no good reason for rebellion against the order which they maintain.

The experience of history supports the conclusion

that power can endure only if it gives and maintains laws within which men enjoy the liberties they regard as more important than life. Not all peoples everywhere and always have had the same conception of their essential liberties. But whatever they regard as their essential liberties, be they the liberties of the Christian West or of the Moslem world, or of the Hindus, or of the Chinese, it is these liberties which must be respected under the law if the power behind the law is to endure. Though the world is shrunken, we must not imagine that any system of identical laws can prevail everywhere. The East and the West have been formed in widely different cultural traditions. But what can prevail everywhere, if the alliance holds together, is the universal law that force must not be arbitrary, but must be exercised in accordance with laws that are open to discussion and are subject to orderly revision.

An order of this kind can endure, not forever in a changing world, but for a long and beneficent period of time. Security and liberty are the benefits which such an order can provide. They are such great benefits that whenever men have enjoyed them at all they have rallied to the authority which provided them. It was because the Roman legions brought with them the Roman law that the Roman Empire lived on so long, and, when it fell, lived on in men's memories for a thousand years as an ideal to which they longed to return. It has been Britain's devotion to law which, despite all the rebellion against British rule, has brought so many nations to Britain's side whenever Britain has been really threatened. And I think Americans may without false pride believe that in the last analysis it is our own preference for liberty under law, and not our material power only, which has made the neighbor republics of this hemisphere believe that their vital interests and ours are the same.

4. Conclusion as to the Organization of a New Order

For these reasons it is self-evident that in a fully enlightened view of the vital interests of the great powers and of the smaller we may conclude that: —

To establish and maintain order the nuclear alliance must be consolidated and perpetuated.

To perpetuate their alliance the great powers must become the organizers of an order in which the other peoples find that their liberties are recognized by laws that the great powers respect and that all peoples are compelled to observe.

If this is done, the new order will rest not on sentiment but on enlightened interest. Then only will it be strong enough to have authority. Then only will it be liberal enough to have its authority persist.

5. *Finale*

The structure of the order which the nuclear allies could or should institute, the laws and covenants they could or should subscribe to, the procedures they could or should agree upon — these matters lie outside the province of this inquiry. We have been concerned with finding the American foreign policy which will most adequately and surely make this republic solvent in its foreign relations. We have, therefore, dwelt upon those measures which are indispensable to America if it is to fulfill the commitments it has, if it is to be able to make commitments at all. We have found, I believe, that the measures which will most securely maintain the vital interests of the United States are measures which will no less securely maintain the vital interests of our neighbors, the great ones and the smaller ones alike.

Guided by this principle, and determined to apply it, we shall be capable again of forming an American foreign policy. We shall no longer be, as we have been for nearly fifty years, without a foreign policy which takes account of our interests. We need no longer be divided because the national interest upon which we must unite will have been made evident to us. We shall no longer exhort mankind to build castles in the air while we build our own defenses on sand.

Then, when we know what we ourselves need and

how we must achieve it, we shall be not only a great power. We shall have become at last a mature power. We shall know our interests and what they require of us. We shall know our limitations and our place in the scheme of things.

Then "we may choose peace or war, as our interest, guided by justice, shall counsel"; then the duty which Washington laid upon us will be done.